THINKING ON PAPER
A GUIDE TO WRITING AND REVISING

THINKING ON PAPER

A GUIDE TO WRITING AND REVISING

Priscilla B. Adams

The Westminster Schools
Atlanta, Georgia

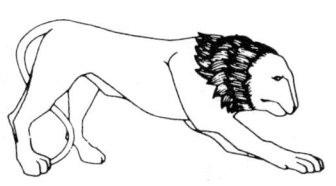

WAYSIDE PUBLISHING
129 Commonwealth Ave
Concord, Ma 01742
(508) 369-2519

Cover design by
G. Gordon Boice

©Independent School Press, Inc., 1985

All rights reserved. No part of this publication may be reproduced or transmitted in any form or by any means, **electronic** or **mechanical,** including **photocopy, recording,** or any **information storage** or retrieval system, without permission in writing from the publisher.

PRINTED IN THE UNITED STATES OF AMERICA.

0–88334-185-9

85868788
12345678

For Larry, Kristen, and Clay,
with whom I have tackled many problems
and discovered many
unexpected gifts.

CONTENTS

SHOPTALK *xv*

Why write? *xv*
Who writes? *xvi*
Where can you get ideas for writing? *xvi*
What are the marks of a good writer? *xvii*
How can you learn to write better? *xix*
How do you use this book? *xx*

EDITOR'S WORKSHOP I: MAKING YOUR PROMISE *1*

Begin at the beginning *1*
Keep an open mind *2*

Touchstones:
 "Foreword," *An Autobiography: Agatha Christie* *2*
 "Foreword," *Great American Deserts,* Edmund C. Jaeger *5*

Honing In *6*
The Critical Angle *8*
Writers at Work *11*

EDITOR'S WORKSHOP II: KEEPING YOUR PROMISE *13*

Be sure you have developed your topic *13*
Composition begins in the body of your paper *14*
Most topics imply specific types of development *15*
Don't tell. Show *19*
Keep in mind the questions you want to answer *19*
Question + Answer = Paragraph *20*

Touchstones and Readings:
  From "The Creative Arts," Louis Kronenberger   *15*
  "Going Beyond Fitness," George Sheehan   *16*
  From "A Child's Christmas in Wales," Dylan
    Thomas   *18*
  Student Essays   *21, 31*
  "The Creative Heritage," Mark Van Doren   *23*
  "The Sea and the Wind That Blows," E. B. White   *27*
  From "The Thrill and Magic of a Country Store,"
    John Parris   *30*
  "The Hobbit (I)" and "The Raven" from *ShrinkLits*,
    Maurice Sagoff   *34*

Honing In   *21*
The Critical Angle   *31*
Writers at Work   *37*

EDITOR'S WORKSHOP III: THE BIG PICTURE   *41*

Three things you should avoid   *41*
Find the right combination   *42*
Keep the main parts in proper perspective   *44*
Maintain order with transitions   *44*
Pay special attention to the ending   *45*

Touchstones:
  "Foreword," *Step by Step Macramé*, Milton
    Sonday   *45*
  "Ogeechee," from *Georgia Rivers*, Andrew Sparks   *46*
  "My Room," Student Essay   *47*
  From "A Child's Christmas in Wales," Dylan
    Thomas   *48*
  From "The Prologue," *The Family of Man*,
    Carl Sandburg   *48*

Honing In *50*
The Critical Angle *53*
Writers at Work *55*

EDITOR'S WORKSHOP IV: CULTIVATING A BECOMING STYLE *63*

Develop word-consciousness *63*
Learn to use the dictionary and a thesaurus *64*
Avoid smokescreens *65*
"Bell's Lettres," Natalie Angier *65*
Read good writing *68*
Borrow from the poets *68*

Touchstones and Readings:
  "The Dreamer," William Childress *69*
  From "A Liberal Education: and Where to Find It,"
    Thomas Henry Huxley *70*
  From "On Slavery," Abraham Lincoln *71*
  From "Reminiscences of Childhood," Dylan
    Thomas *72*
  From "A Christmas Memory," Truman Capote *78*
  From *Great Expectations*, Charles Dickens *80*

Honing In *79*
The Critical Angle *81*
Writers at Work *83*

EDITOR'S WORKSHOP V: AVOIDING MECHANICAL BREAKDOWNS *99*

Incomplete sentence (fragment) *100*
Run-on sentence *100*
Inconsistency in the use of pronouns and verbs *101*
Errors in capitalization *103*

Misspelled words and confused homonyms *103*
Punctuation errors *104*
   The Dash *105*
   Underlining *105*
   Quotation Marks *105*
   The Comma *106*
   Parentheses *106*
   The Semicolon *107*
   The Colon *107*
   The Apostrophe *107*

Touchstones:
   From *Flowers for Algernon,* Daniel Keyes *104*
   "Shawn on Ross," from *Here at the New Yorker,*
     Brendan Gill *108*

Honing In *110*
The Critical Angle *110*

WRITER TO WRITER *115*

   Improving through sharing *115*
   Putting your old papers to work *117*
   Understanding what the grade means *119*

ACKNOWLEDGMENTS

Grateful acknowledgment is made to the following publishers, authors, and students for permission to use excerpts from their works:

To Harcourt Brace Jovanovich, Inc. for excerpt from "The Function of Criticism" and excerpt from "The Metaphysical Poets" appearing in *Selected Essays* by T. S. Eliot, copyright © 1960, and for excerpts from *Flowers for Algernon*, copyright ©1959, 1966 by Daniel Keyes. Reprinted by permission of Harcourt Brace Jovanovich, Inc.

To Saturday Review Magazine Corporation for excerpts from "Thoughts on Literature" by Norman Cousins and from "Creators on Creating: Robert Penn Warren" by Carll Tucker, July 1981 issue, copyright © 1981 by *Saturday Review*. All rights reserved. Reprinted by permission.

To Harper & Row, Publishers, Inc. for excerpt from *Letters Home* by Aurelia Schober Plath, copyright © 1975 by Aurelia Schober Plath. Reprinted by permission of Harper & Row, Publishers, Inc. and for excerpt from *Essays of E. B. White* by E. B. White. Copyright © 1963 by E. B. White. Reprinted by permission of Harper & Row Publishers, Inc.

To Dodd, Mead & Company, Inc. for the Foreword from *An Autobiography: Agatha Christie*. Reprinted by permission of Dodd, Mead & Company, Inc. Copyright © 1977 by Agatha Christie Limited.

To National Geographic Society for the Foreword by Edmund C. Jaeger from the Society's special publication *Great American Deserts,* by Rowe Findley.

To Mrs. Louis Kronenberger for permission to use excerpt from the article "The Creative Arts" by Louis Kronenberger.

To Runner's World Magazine Company, Inc. for "Going Beyond Fitness" by George Sheehan, from the 1974 publication of *The Complete Runner* (World Publications, Inc.).

To New Directions Publishing Corporation for excerpts from Dylan Thomas, *Quite Early One Morning*. Copyright © 1954 by New Directions Publishing Corporation. Reprinted by permission of New Directions Publishing Corporation.

To Citizen-Times Publishing Company for excerpt from "The Thrill and Magic of a Country Store" by John Parris. Excerpt taken from *These Storied Mountains*.

To Workman Publishing Company for excerpts from *ShrinkLits,* copyright © 1970, 1980 by Maurice Sagoff. Workman Publishing Company, New York. Reprinted with permission of the publisher.

To Western Publishing Company, Inc. for excerpt from *Step by Step Macramé* by Mary Walker Phillips, copyright © 1970 by Western Publishing Company, Inc. Reprinted by permission.

To the Atlanta Journal and Constitution Magazine, August 13, 1961 for permission to reprint essay entitled "Ogeechee" by Andrew Sparks.

To the Museum of Modern Art, New York, for permission to use excerpts from the Prologue by Carl Sandburg to *The Family of Man* edited by Edward Stiechen. Copyright © 1955, The Museum of Modern Art, New York. All rights reserved. Reprinted by permission of the publisher.

To Discover Magazine for permission to use excerpts. Natalie Angier, copyright © 1981 Discover Magazine, Time Inc.

To William Childress for permission to reprint "The Dreamer" and his comments on writing it.

To Random House, Inc. for permission to use excerpt from "A Christmas Memory" by Truman Capote. Copyright © 1965 by Truman Capote. Reprinted from *Breakfast at Tiffany's* by Truman Capote, by permission of Random House, Inc. and excerpt from *Here at the New Yorker,* by Brendan Gill. Copyright © 1975 by Brendan Gill. Reprinted by permission of Random House, Inc.

To Resources for American Literary Study for permission to reprint excerpt from "A Chat with Willa Cather" by Floyd C. Watkins and John T. Hiers, Spring 1979 issue.

To Professor Floyd C. Watkins and the staff of the Special Collections division of Woodruff Library at Emory University, Atlanta, Georgia, for permission to use material from Dr. Watkins's manuscripts.

To University of Georgia Press for permission to reprint excerpts from *In Time and Place: Some Origins of American Fiction* by Floyd C. Watkins, Copyright 1977, and from *Yesterday in the Hills* by Floyd C. Watkins and Charles Hubert Watkins, copyright 1973, 1982.

To many students, past and present, of The Westminster Schools, Atlanta, Georgia; but especially to Stephen Ahn, Courtney Cook, Harriet Daugherty, Tim Hanes, Jeff Hyde, Marc Lipsitch, Archie Roberts, Michael Rubenstein, and Abbott Whitney.

To Dr. John Roberts and Nedra Pezold Roberts, The Westminster Schools, and Marguerite A. Davis, Independent School Press, for their valuable suggestions and enthusiastic support.

Shoptalk

Why write? Why write when there are more expedient ways to communicate? Speech and gestures are more spontaneous. Why not use them instead? Write because writing is thinking on paper and because your best writing is the result of your soundest thinking. It is because you can control and deliberate over your choice of words that what you write is significant and valuable to your reader.

Conversation and gestures come easily because they rush forth out of the impulse to voice our thoughts immediately. Although these are equally as important as a means of communication, they cannot take the place of writing. While speakers in dialogue respond to each other's words and gestures, the writer engages a silent partner in dialogue; a partner whose moods and needs and thoughts must be anticipated and for whom the writer must carefully choose words in response.

Write also because for some time to come it will be the major way in which you reveal what you know. You will not be able to graduate from any institution without first validating that you have learned what you were supposed to have learned; that validation is almost always done through writing. Write because writing will continue to be the method of expression you will most often use when you have taken a job after graduation. Most jobs involve some written reports, proposals, memoranda, letters and order forms, and writing them is just another way of validating what you know.

Control, precision, permanence, truth made clear and preserved for others to reflect on—these are the goals the writer seeks to accomplish. Journalists, historians, lawyers, theologians, public officials, scientists, sales managers, police officers, engineers—all writers—set down the truth as they see it. Writers write to set the record straight, whether their writing takes the form of a letter, a book, a proposal, a report, a law, an article, a speech, minutes, memos, or sermons. The form the writer selects is chosen carefully to match the purpose of the writing and the audience to which it is directed; the goal—however varied the purpose, the audience or the form—is a singular one: to tell the truth.

Who writes? Anyone writes who wants so earnestly to communicate an idea to someone else that he or she is willing to take the time to think through just what idea or ideas are to be conveyed to the reader and figure out how the message can be put across. Of course, we learn as we write, and we have a sense of self-satisfaction as we do it, but the most rewarding aspect of writing is sharing it with someone else. In other words, any one of us may be justifiably classified as "a writer" when we make the effort to be one. A writer is not, by virtue of being a student or of practicing a particular profession, a member of a select group to which the rest of us may not belong.

Where can you get ideas for writing? A writer draws from the commonplace experiences of life. Even in our academic communities, we have a specific body of common experiences: things happen on the way to school, at school, after school, and on the weekend. At school, for example, we go to the same assemblies, look out the same windows, eat in the same cafeteria. A good writer not only verbalizes in an articulate fashion personal thoughts about these common experiences, but also voices the thoughts of others. The good writer is able to process commonplace events into a whole experience; to draw away from the experience in order to become a critical observer of it and to reach conclusions or share certain observations.

As a result, those of us who share commonplace experiences will see them in a new light because of the way the writing affects us. When critic T. S. Eliot described how the mind of the poet voices our commonplace experiences, he emphasized the writer's role in making us see truth more clearly:

> When a poet's mind is perfectly equipped for its work, it is constantly amalgamating disparate experience; the ordinary man's experience is chaotic, irregular, fragmentary. The latter falls in love or reads Spinoza, and these two have nothing to do with each other, or with the noise of the typewriter or the smell of cooking; in the mind of the poet these experiences are always forming new wholes.
>
> "The Metaphysical Poets"

Norman Cousins, Editor Emeritus of *Saturday Review,* described the writer's art this way:

> The writer's art is measured by the ability to transcend personal memory. The function of a writer is to widen the path to the subconscious, to awaken memories of the race, to refine the ability of an individual to have contact with life, to be at one with others.
>
> "Thoughts on Literature"

What are the marks of a good writer? The good writer is one who has either voiced our thoughts or who has made us understand his or hers. We react to good writing by saying to ourselves, "How clear this is!" or, "How many times have I felt or thought or seen this!"

A noted "good writer" is Sylvia Plath, author of *The Bell Jar* and *Ariel*. She wrote the following entry in her diary when she was a student. Her direct and informal style is characteristic of the free-writing stage in which most composing begins. Her goal is primarily to set down the truth about herself, but, of course, her concerns are those many teenagers may share:

> As of today I have decided to keep a diary again—just a place where I can write my thoughts and opinions when I have a moment. Somehow I have to keep and hold the rapture of being seventeen. Every day is so precious I feel infinitely sad at the thought of all this time melting farther and farther away from me as I grow older. *Now, now* is the perfect time of my life.
>
> In reflecting back upon these last sixteen years, I can see tragedies and happiness, all relative—all unimportant now—fit only to smile upon a bit mistily.
>
> I still do not know myself. Perhaps I never will. But I feel free—unbound by responsibility, I still can come up to my own private room, with my drawings hanging on the walls . . . and pictures pinned up over my bureau. It is a room suited to me—tailored, uncluttered and peaceful. . . . I love the quiet lines of the furniture, the two bookcases filled with poetry books and fairy tales saved from childhood.
>
> At the present moment I am very happy, sitting at my desk, looking out at the bare trees around the house across the street. . . . Always I want to be an observer. I want to be affected by life deeply, but never so blinded that I cannot see my share of existence in a wry, humorous light and mock myself as I mock others.

I am afraid of getting older. I am afraid of getting married. Spare me from cooking three meals a day—spare me from the relentless cage of routine and rote. I want to be free—free to know people and their backgrounds—free to move to different parts of the world so I may learn that there are other morals and standards besides my own. I want, I think, to be omniscient . . . I think I would like to call myself "The girl who wanted to be God." Yet if I were not in this body, where *would* I be—perhaps I am *destined* to be classified and qualified. But, oh, I cry out against it. I am I—I am powerful—but to what extent? I am I.

Sometimes I try to put myself in another's place, and I am frightened when I find I am almost succeeding. How awful to be anyone but I. I have a terrible egotism. I love my flesh, my face, my limbs with overwhelming devotion. I know that I am "too tall" and have a fat nose, and yet I pose and prink before the mirror, seeing more and more how lovely I am . . . I have erected in my mind an image of myself—idealistic and beautiful. Is not that image, free from blemish, the true self—the true perfection? Am I wrong when this image insinuates itself between me and the merciless mirror? (Oh, even now I glance back on what I have just written—how foolish it sounds, how overdramatic.)

Never, never, never will I reach the perfection I long for with all my soul—my paintings, my poems, my stories—all poor, poor reflections . . . for I have been too thoroughly conditioned to the conventional surroundings of this community . . . my vanity desires luxuries which I can never have. . . .

I am continually more aware of the power which chance plays in my life. . . . There will come a time when I must face myself at last. Even now I dread the big choices which loom up in my life—what college? What career? I am afraid. I feel uncertain. What is best for me? What do I want? I do not know. I love freedom. I deplore constrictions and limitations. . . . I am not as wise as I have thought. I can now see, as from a valley, the roads lying open for me, but I cannot see the end—the consequences. . . .

Oh, I love *now,* with all my fears and forebodings, for *now* I still am not completely molded. My life is still just beginning. I am strong. I long for a cause to devote my energies to. . . .

Letters Home

A good writer can also see commonplace experience with someone else's eyes. He or she can look at our school lives, for instance, from the point of view of a teacher nearing retirement, an undistinguished student, an aging former football star, an alumnus remembering "the good old days," or the valedictorian nearing graduation. The good writer naturally assumes the posture and the voice that each of the different persons would understand and use because careful thought has been given to the likelihood that a particular audience would be receptive to that voice.

The good writer never forgets the silent partner in dialogue—the reader. Without the reader, writing is virtually sterile; its only value is in the release of emotion that writing it has given the writer. A journal or diary entry is intended to be used in this way. For the most part, the writing that you do will be intentional; that is, it will be directed to someone or to some group in particular. The poor thinker often uses the expression "you know what I mean" to shift the burden onto another person to find the right words to express what he or she is thinking and feeling. That request is impossible to fulfill; only you know what you mean to say and if it is important enough to you to get your message across—and to a good writer it is—then you will search until you have found precisely what will elicit the desired response from the particular audience you have in mind. The good writer is sensitive to the reader; you are exhibiting this trait when you choose the appropriate voice, tone, and diction for any piece of writing, whether it is an article for the school newspaper, a letter or a note to a friend, or a report to be used in the classroom.

How can you learn to write better? Since most writing is intended to communicate, the energy you use to write will be wasted unless you have thought clearly enough on paper to communicate what you intended. The key to writing better is in knowing what to look for to be sure you have communicated the right message; knowing what to look for means knowing how to revise. In fact, the word *revise* itself means "to see again" and the purpose of this book is to show just how one revises or takes a closer look at his or her writing.

If you have been writing compositions for some time, you may already know how to proofread; this is a necessary step, but it is a final and a basically cosmetic one in which one catches careless errors. Proofreading cannot be used as a substitute for revision. Revision is the step in which the very fabric of the paper is examined: the content, the organization, the tone, the point of view, and other major considerations.

How do you use this book? *Thinking on Paper* is intended to help you sharpen your editing skills and will prevent you from making useless attempts to improve your papers. Simply copying them over with neater handwriting or more careful attention to the width of the margins will not automatically improve the quality of the writing. This book will guide you through the steps of the writing process and will show you what to look for all along the way as you write and revise. Further, once you have written a rough draft, it will help you see more clearly the whole picture your composition presents.

The book is divided into five **Editor's Workshops,** each of which focuses on a separate step of the writing process. Within each of these are three sections: *Touchstones, Honing In,* and *The Critical Angle.*

Touchstones ◾ are the works of good writers, both students and professionals, to be used as a jeweler uses a touchstone, to identify and set standards of excellence.

Following these are short exercises for *Honing In* → ←. Just as a whetstone is used to sharpen a precision instrument, these exercises will help you sharpen a specific skill by using it in a brief writing assignment or by judging the effectiveness with which another writer has used it.

The Critical Angle ◢ ◤ section of each **Workshop** will be a culminating assignment that will require the writing, planning, or revision of a full draft of a composition using the major skill on which the **Workshop** is based. It is so named because in optics the term *critical angle* refers to the point at which total reflection takes place, and to complete these assignments will require careful reflection and precise judgment.

At the conclusion of the **Workshops** are the Writers at Work. These sections contain preliminary drafts of student compositions and pages from the works of professional authors as they were in the process of revising. They show ways to solve the composition problems most writers are likely to encounter.

THINKING ON PAPER
A GUIDE TO WRITING AND REVISING

Probably, indeed, the larger part of the labour of an author in composing his work is critical labour; the labour of sifting, combining, constructing, expunging, correcting, testing: this frightful toil is as much critical as creative. I maintain even that the criticism employed by a trained and skilled writer on his own work is the most vital, the highest kind of criticism; and (as I think I have said before) that some creative writers are superior to others solely because their critical faculty is superior.

           T. S. Eliot
           "The Function of Criticism"

Editor's Workshop I: Making Your Promise

Your first writing efforts are just that—efforts. They serve no other purpose than to warm you up to your subject and to your audience. You can polish the second or third time around, but, at first, just free-write your thoughts as you would tell them to a friend in a letter or in a conversation. Be as direct, as spontaneous, and as informal as you would be in these instances.

Begin at the beginning. Begin by stressing what you are writing about and why you are writing about it. Then explain why you think your reader will be interested in what you have to say. For instance, are you writing to make a point and to persuade a certain individual or group to believe as you do? Are you writing to explain a process or an idea to someone who needs to know more about it? Are you writing in order to describe a place or a person in a really clear way?

Beginning your paper by stressing your purpose and your subject will help you find a *focus* for your writing. Once you've found it, you will be well on your way to writing the more precise statement about it that will appear in the finished paper as your *thesis*. You need to know the general direction your paper may take long before you decide on its precise nature.

Think of this free-writing stage as the time you spend deciding on the nature of a promise you are making to the reader, a kind of contract in which the terms are spelled out: what you intend to tell, why the reader needs to know this, and what you expect the response to be. Remember that writing is a dialogue between reader and writer; good writers never forget that the only reason for writing anything is the expectation that it will be read and evaluated and will prompt someone to take action. Do not expect your reader to guess why he or she should read what you have written. *Show* the reader. *Tell* the reader. This part of the writing process ensures that you yourself know why.

Keep an open mind. You may find as the paper progresses that it is impossible to fulfill the promise you made. That the writer has not followed through or cannot follow through on even the best intentions is the kind of revelation every *good* writer has now and then; it is precisely the kind of revelation that rarely comes naturally to the poor writer. The poor writer waits for the teacher or for another reader to point out that the goals set have not been accomplished.

If you find later that you have not taken the direction you set out to take, your choice is either to recognize that you have misstated the purpose and to restate the purpose as that which you have, in fact, accomplished; or, if you feel that you have gotten off-track and do not wish to pursue this direction, eliminate the off-track material and start over. The revelation that you have been diverted from your true purpose is the beginning of the kind of wisdom that will result in *structural,* as opposed to *cosmetic,* revisions of your paper. The original focus is important because you must periodically hold it up to your paper as you would a mirror, to see if it is reflected in the rest of the paper.

The following are forewords from two different types of books. Each author has addressed the basic issues of subject and purpose before presenting the body of the work, just as you must address them before you present the body of your composition. Read the forewords carefully, picking out the passages that make clear the "what" and "why" of each work that is to follow. What has been the role of personal experience in shaping the focus of each of the works?

✺ *Touchstone:* "Foreword," *An Autobiography: Agatha Christie*

I ought to be writing a detective story, but with the writer's natural urge to write anything but what he should be writing, I long, quite unexpectedly, to write my autobiography. The urge to write one's autobiography, so I have been told, overtakes everyone sooner or later. It has suddenly overtaken me!

On second thoughts, autobiography is much too grand a word. It suggests a purposeful study of one's whole life. It implies names, dates and places in tidy chronological order. What I want is to plunge my hand into a lucky dip and come up with a handful of assorted memories.

Life seems to me to consist of three parts: the absorbing and usually enjoyable present, which rushes on from minute to minute with fatal speed; the future, dim and uncertain, for which one can make any number of interesting plans, the wilder and more improbable the better, since—as nothing will turn out as you expect it to do—you might as well have the fun of planning anyway; and thirdly, the past, the memories and realities that are the bedrock of one's present life, brought back to you suddenly by a scent, the shape of a hill, an old song—some triviality that makes one suddenly say "I remember" with a peculiar and quite unexplainable pleasure.

This is one of the compensations that age brings, and certainly a very enjoyable one—to remember.

Unfortunately you often wish not only to remember, but also to talk about what you remember. And this, you have to tell yourself repeatedly, is boring for other people. Why should they be interested in what, after all, is *your* life, not theirs? They do, occasionally, when young, accord to you a certain historical curiosity.

"I suppose," a well-educated (?) young girl says with interest, "that you remember *all* about the Crimea?"

Rather hurt, I reply acidly that I'm not quite as old as that. I also repudiate participation in the Indian Mutiny. But I admit to recollections of the Boer War—I should, my brother fought in it.

But I will confess that the first memory that springs up in my mind is a clear picture of myself walking along the streets of Dinard on market day with my mother—a boy with a great basket of stuff cannons roughly into me, grazing my arm and nearly knocking me flat. It hurts. I begin to cry. I am, I think, about seven years old.

My mother, who likes stoic behavior in public places, remonstrates with me.

"Think," she says, "of our brave soldiers in South Africa."

In the interests of truth I have shamefully to admit that my answer is to bawl out:

"I don't want to be a brave soldier. I want to be a coward!"

What governs one's choice of memories? Life is very like sitting in a cinema. Flick! Here am I, a child eating eclairs on my birthday. Flick! Two years have passed and here I am sitting on my grandmother's lap, being solemnly trussed up as a chicken just arrived from Mr. Whiteley's, and almost hysterical with the wit of the joke.

Just moments—and in between long empty spaces of months or even years. Where was one then? It brings home to one Peer Gynt's question: "Where was I, myself, the whole man, the true man?"

We never know the whole man, though sometimes, in quick flashes, we know the true man. I think, myself, that one's memories represent those moments which, insignificant as they may seem, nevertheless represent the inner self and oneself as most really oneself.

I am today the same person as that solemn little girl with pale flaxen sausage curls. The house in which the spirit dwells; grows, develops instincts and tastes and emotions and intellectual capacities, but I myself, the true Agatha, am the same. I do not know the whole Agatha. The whole Agatha, so I believe, is known only to God.

So there we are, all of us, little Agatha Miller, and big Agatha Miller, and Agatha Christie and Agatha Mallowan proceeding on our way—where? That one doesn't know—which, of course, makes life exciting. I have always thought life exciting and I still do.

Because one knows so little of it—only one's own tiny part—one is like an actor who has a few lines to say in Act I. He has a typewritten script with his cues, and that is all that he can know. He hasn't read the play. Why should he? His but to say "The telephone is out of order, madam" and then retire into obscurity.

But when the curtain goes up on the day of performance, he will hear the play through, and he will be there to line up with the rest, and take his call.

To be part of something one doesn't in the least understand is, I think, one of the most intriguing things about life.

I like living. I have sometimes been wildly despairing, acutely miserable, racked with sorrow, but through it all, I still know quite certainly that just to be alive is a grand thing.

So what I plan to do is to enjoy the pleasures of memory—not hurrying myself—writing a few pages from time to time. It is a task that will probably go on for years. But why do I call it a *task?* It is as if it's an indulgence. I once saw an old Chinese scroll that I loved. It had an old man sitting under a tree playing cat's cradle. It was called "Old Man enjoying the pleasures of Idleness." I've never forgotten it.

So having settled that I'm going to enjoy myself, I had better, perhaps, begin. And though I don't expect to be able to keep up a chronological continuity, I can at least try to begin at the beginning.

✱ *Touchstone:* "Foreword," *Great American Deserts,*
Edmund C. Jaeger

For 65 years now I have loved the desert. I first saw it from the windows of a train, traveling from Nebraska to California with my parents. My father needed a change of climate for his health. It was 1906, the year of the San Francisco earthquake, and the ground was still trembling there when we reached California. Of the desert we crossed I remember wide expanses of creosote bush, great sandy washes, and Indians standing on the platform at Yuma.

A few year later, when I was still a young man, I climbed more than 10,000 feet to the peak of Mount San Jacinto and saw the desert spread below me. I felt its vastness and solitude—and beauty—tugging at me, and I vowed then and there that one day I would know it. For 30 years I was a Professor of Zoology at City College in Riverside, California, and I spent nearly every weekend and holiday camping in the desert with my students.

I remember campsites rimmed with beds of sand verbenas and evening primroses, smoke tree washes and sage-brush valleys. I remember riding a burro into Palm Springs, at the edge of the desert, where I began teaching. There were 40 registered voters there, mostly Indians. Now, of course, it's a plush resort. And I remember waking at dawn and seeing a coyote playing with a piece of canvas from our camping equipment, tossing it and tugging it, frolicking like a puppy. He ran right across the chest of my sleeping companion and began cavorting with some crumpled wastepaper we were saving for our morning fire. He was not in the least bothered by our presence. I have great admiration for the coyote, for in spite of all persecutions of man, and all the hardships he must endure, still he thrives.

Water is the life of the desert. There are desert animals that never need a drink of water. There are desert seeds that can wait 15 to 20 years for rainfall. That to me is one of the wonders of life. A seed no larger than a period on this page can hold all of a plant's possibilities, waiting. No thinking man can fail to be awed by the mystery of it.

There is only one way really to see the desert, and that is on foot, away from the highways. The desert of people is not my desert. I want open space. I want to see the animals and flowers of the desert, to hear the sounds of the dry, whistling winds, and the insects and the birds. The desert is largely a land of silence, but if you listen you can hear it.

I'm glad that I've lived during the period that I have, for I saw the deserts in their pristine state. All my life I have enjoyed the boundless solitude and space. In just the past 30 years, huge areas of desert lands, watered by man-made reservoirs and opened by roads, have become home to millions. Many have exploited the deserts as a source of quick riches from minerals, land speculation, overbuilding, careless recreation. While it seems inevitable that desert areas will be put to man's physical use more and more in the next decades, I hope some significant portion will be preserved in its natural state for the soul of man. This intelligent and perceptive book should help inspire us toward that goal. Just as deserts have long been a source of great joy to me, I know they can be for thousands of others. We need only approach them on their own terms—and with great reverence.

→ *Honing In* ←

Assignment 1:

The following two examples are the introductory paragraphs of student-written compositions. Examine each of them carefully. What is the subject of each paper? Why is each student writing about the topic he or she has chosen? What response are you expected to make to the writing? What do you think the rest of the compositions will be about?

Introduction A:

When I am in my room, I am surrounded by symbols of myself. They remind me daily who and what I am. I can see clearly that my room is mine because it is an extension of my separate selves. It symbolizes not only my private self, but also my public, and even my imagined self as well.

Introduction B:

As I sit in this old building, Wilton High School, I am aware of its proud history and my attachment to it. I have grown with this school, so she is special to me. When I graduate in June, I will be leaving behind something that will be hard to replace. Here I have made friendships, almost since the beginning of my life. There are people here—students and teachers—who know me almost as well as I know myself.

Assignment 2:

Announcements of various kinds abound in most schools and reading and writing them provides an excellent opportunity to practice identifying a focus and a purpose. An effective announcement is *specific, complete,* and *brief.* Furthermore, it must be presented in an interesting format or it may be ignored. Prepare an announcement for an activity that meets the foregoing criteria. In addition, copy or bring a facsimile of an announcement you have seen, heard, or read. Point out the degree to which it meets the standards of clarity mentioned above. Suggest appropriate revisions where it fails to do so.

As you begin to search for a focus and a purpose, you, like Agatha Christie and Edmund Jaeger, must take seriously that you write best about what you know best. What are the major areas in which you have personal experience or first-hand knowledge? The number is probably more than you would guess. A few areas are listed below.

1. *Yourself:* a childhood memory; something that angers, interests, frightens, troubles, or excites you; something you value; something you dream of making or doing; something you'd like to change or see changed; personal likes or dislikes.

2. *Other people:* your best friend; your greatest rival or "enemy;" the members of your family; your teachers; a person you admire.

3. *Places you've been:* your home, your school, your town or community; your neighborhood; your church; vacation spots.

4. *Things you've seen:* sporting events; movies; plays; television shows.

5. *Things you've read:* newspapers; books; posters; pamphlets; letters; magazines; yearbooks.

You might, of course, write a paper in which you simply develop each of these interests briefly, but the result would be an ineffective piece of writing that would be no more than a collection of thoughts or ideas about various subjects. It would be ineffective writing because it would not have a focus. The following series of steps is designed to help you see how writers work at finding their true purposes.

◢ *The Critical Angle* ◣

Step 1: From one of the five areas in which you have experience, pick out a sub-category and then list under it several random thoughts or impressions that come to mind when you think of that topic. Your first efforts at finding a focus might be like this:

<u>School</u>
getting a date the day before the dance
forgetting the combination to my lock
yelling so loudly at the pep rally before the homecoming game that I couldn't speak a word at the game
making a "C" on the history paper I thought I "aced"
seeing Mr. Holloway on his way home the day I was "sick"

<u>My Personal Likes and Dislikes</u>
love sports, never made any varsity team
like green because it's the school color and looks well with my blonde hair
like food, especially Mom's brownies
like to experiment in the kitchen
like phys. ed. and biology best of all subjects
have strong opinions about some things: the dress code, music, my religion, algebra

Of course, your random list might continue indefinitely, but eventually the items on it will begin to present an overall impression or pattern based on your observations about the topic.

Step 2: After you have made a fairly exhaustive list, study it carefully and see if you can think of three or four questions that are answered by the items on the list. For instance, if you had made the list above on school, your impressions might have answered the following questions:

1. What are these "best years of my life" really like? (frustrating, disappointing, active)
2. What kind of relationship do I have with my peers? (lost-in-the crowd, reticent student)

> 3. What are the real lessons I've learned at school?
>   (cultivate self-discipline, be honest, get involved)

The list of your likes and dislikes might have answered the following questions:

> 1. What do I seem to be interested in?
>   (sports, cooking, religion)
> 2. What kind of personality do I have
>   (self-assured, ambitious)
> 3. What kind of dreams do I have?
>   (career in modeling, medicine)

Step 3: Next, write each of your questions on a separate index card or sheet of notebook paper and answer it as fully as you can, writing in full sentences. Use ideas from your list wherever they seem appropriate.

Step 4: Study the questions and answers to see what direction your paper might take. Then, following the guidelines given at the beginning of this chapter, under *Begin at the beginning* and *Keep an open mind*, write two different opening paragraphs for a paper on this subject, stressing the subject and the purpose. Follow the examples set by the two *Touchstone* forewords. Create interesting enough paragraphs to make the reader want to read the rest of what you have to say. You may even want to indicate how the rest of the paper will be organized.

Step 5: Have your teacher and another student or two read your questions and answers and indicate which of your two introductory paragraphs best addresses the true subject and purpose that the questions indicate they should. Save both the best introduction and the questions and answers for use in a later stage of the process, which will be covered in the next **Workshop**.

Writers at Work

From "Every Christmas" by Tim Hanes, student

  A paper without an introduction or a conclusion is an enigma to the reader. It is as if one has been invited to eavesdrop on a discussion already in progress and finds the invitation suddenly withdrawn before discovering what the discussion is all about. This composition has only one sentence of introduction, and it is affixed to the first paragraph of the body.

Every Christmas

  Every Christmas is an ordeal for our family. One of the traditions we have long held is getting the tree. Every year we children argue that the tree should be purchased early. And every year Mom and Dad argue that we have plenty of time. Usually the children win, and to our dismay, Christmas arrives long after all the needles on the tree have departed.

  There is, of course, the matter of deciding what kind of tree to get, once we get around to buying it. Dad and the older children want a cut tree, while Mom and the younger ones want a live one. Dad and his group usually win, but one year we did get a live tree. After Christmas, we planted it in the backyard; it died almost immediately, but we left it in the yard, hoping that it would sprout unexpectedly. In the back yard it remained, until one day Chris, my oldest brother, knocked it over when he accidentally leaned on it.

Here is the introductory paragraph that appeared on Tim's final draft. He omitted the first sentence altogether, and chose instead to explain the nature of the memories contained in the paper:

Christmas seems to harbor more memories than any other period of the year. My family, like all families, has its own special kind of Christmas celebration. Every one follows the same pattern. Most of my Christmas memories are vivid, but others come from recollections my family has shared with me.

Editor's Workshop II: Keeping Your Promise

Writing is a unique form of communication. You write your message and send it out to stand on its own merits. Your readers do not have you present to clarify matters and you cannot depend on them for cues. You must anticipate as nearly as possible their reactions to your message. The thinking process required of a good writer is different from that required of a good speaker or of someone who can brainstorm a singular idea.

Poor writers do not know that a writing process exists. Many of them are embarrassed to admit that when they sit down and write, they turn out unacceptable writing. The truth is that most people who simply sit down and write produce poor writing; even good thinkers and good conversationalists produce poor writing when they do it this way. Poor writers think their writing is bad because something is wrong with them, but the only thing wrong is the notion that one can produce good writing without attempting to improve on or *develop* one's first efforts.

Development is not a mysterious new skill that is difficult to master. If you choose to write a paper about something you know about or have learned about, then you should be able to discuss the subject thoroughly on paper. When the discussion is cogent and coherent, then the topic has been sufficiently developed. Insufficient topic development occurs when the body of the paper does not adequately fulfill the promise made to the reader in the opening paragraphs. You should not give your reader an editorial or an advertisement in the body when your introduction led him or her to expect an objective report or a detailed description. Topic development is the most serious task facing the beginning writer. If a paper fails to follow through on its opening promise, the paper is a failure, no matter how interesting the details, how perfect the grammar, how impressive the vocabulary.

Be sure you have developed your topic sufficiently. First, try to imagine the faces of your readers, to see them in your mind's eye as persons who want to be shown and told. Try to gauge realistically their levels of interest and balance them against the complexity of the topic. Almost any topic can be treated in papers of varying lengths, according to the needs and interests of the intended readers. Second, in light of these needs and interests, examine your opening promise. Have you proved your opening assertion? Explained your theories? Described specific persons and places accurately? If so, you have adequately developed your topic.

In **Workshop I**, you accumulated details with a specific format in mind—that of a personal theme—and you applied a purpose to it, such as to convince, to inform, to amuse, or to impress. We called this step in the writing process finding a *focus* and it resulted in an introductory paragraph for a paper you could write on the topic you chose. The process of *development* begins after you have the purpose and the format in mind; it begins when the writer considers how to answer the following questions: (1) What do I know about the topic I have chosen? and (2) How do I know what I know? (If you know what convinced you to think the way you do, then you'll start the development process on the right track. You'll be able to use the same method that convinced you in order to convince other people.)

Composition begins in the body, or development portion, of your paper. Composition is a term used to describe similar processes in art and music, as well as in writing. It refers to the harmonious placement of separate entities—notes, colors, ideas—so that they present a pleasing whole—songs, pictures, papers. If the parts are not *composed*, then you do not have a piece of music or art or literature, but rather an unharmonious collection of sounds, colors, or ideas. Furthermore, if the body of your paper does not develop your ideas *harmoniously*, your reader will be unlikely to consider your purpose fulfilled.

Often writers who have not done the necessary pre-writing, thinking and research will resort to platitudes and generalities in an effort to conceal lack of content. But, inevitably, such writers fool only themselves. Neither a character nor an idea can be labelled simply "good" or "bad" and passed off successfully as such to the reader. Both must be developed as a matter of insuring the writer's credibility to the reader through the use of examples, statistics, descriptive details, and other convincing data.

Most topics imply specific types of development. The type of development you use is determined by the topic you have chosen, the kind of material you have gathered, and the guiding purpose you have contracted with the reader to fulfill. One of the tasks in the development stage is discovering which means is appropriate for your specific paper, as in the following examples: 1) If you are preparing a report, your main method of development is likely to be *listing*, with some occasional *identification* or *explanation* of issues. 2) If your primary purpose is to record a singularly important event as accurately as possible, then your methods would likely be *narration* and *description*. 3) If you have chosen to defend a certain position in a controversial matter—something you'd like to see changed or accomplished or prohibited—then your methods might include *reasons, facts, causes and effects,* and *comparisons and contrasts.* 4) If you are explaining the process of making or doing something, you might clarify its *significance* and enumerate *steps*. 5) If you are reacting to a literary work, your methods might be *classification, analysis,* and *summarization.* 6) If your purpose is to delineate a specific character in a literary work, then your methods might be *description* and *example.*

★ *Touchstone:* from "The Creative Arts" by Louis Kronenberger

The first paragraph of the following excerpt is developed with *examples;* the second paragraph is developed with *examples in contrasting pairs:*

> In one sense, the United States has been the most tirelessly "creative" nation in history. No other has been so given to creating new appliances, devising short cuts, contriving fresh angles. Consider our achievements in slang, or in showmanship, or in amusements; think what we have done just to advance the sandwich: club, combination, triple-decker, ice-cream, hero. Think how, since wigwam days, we have varied our habitations, right on to the skyscraping and the split level, the trailer home on wheels, the trail blazer's over a waterfall. Dismiss, if you will, a hundred useful thoughts like the bottle cap, there remain the telegraph, the telephone, the electric light. Ignore miniature golf and drive-in movies, poker remains, and baseball and basketball, and jazz.
>
> Along such largely unaesthetic lines, it's all too easy, of course, to say that we have created all too little. Yet, as creatively

16   *Thinking on Paper*

no nation has shown a more public or social face, none has shown one more private and solitary—Thoreaus and Hawthornes, Emily Dickinsons and Ryders. If we have instituted the public-address system, we have all but perfected the private language; against a Coney Island must be set a Walden Pond; against bumper-to-bumper traffic emerge death on a pale horse, a whaling vessel's crazed captain, a doomed Negro adrift in West Indian waters, an enshuttered spinster in an Amherst house. If we are notorious for our conformists, we have long been proverbial for our cranks; if we everlastingly make pacts with Mammon, we constantly seek peace from God.

✯ *Touchstone:* "Going Beyond Fitness," Dr. George Sheehan, from *The Complete Runner*

Dr. Sheehan would like to see interest in sports and exercise be part of a life-long pursuit of health and well-being. He defends it as esssential to "the good life" in the essay that follows with *reasons* why it should be; he *explains* why the motivation for pursuing healthful activities has not developed naturally.

Most recreational directors, physical education instructors, and promoters of exercise-for-your-health programs feel much the same as the fellow who finds it difficult to give away five dollar bills down Main Street. People just won't believe it's for real.

The programs they prescribe seem so sensible and so in keeping with our nature it is incredible that people don't accept them. But facts are facts and there is no use railing against them. If the plane won't fly, there's no use appealing that the blueprints said it would. A bridge that insists on collapsing in defiance to all engineering theory will not respond to oaths and imprecations. Nor will our neighbors bestir themselves to physical activity unless we find the proper approach to the problem.

This approach will have to go back to basics. Where did we go wrong and how can we fight it? How can men be motivated to do what's good for them? Motivation is the main factor in the continuation of any activity, and especially in adult athletics where there is no longer the need to continue in compulsory school exercise and sports activity. Indeed it is just that transition period from school to work and marriage which carries with it the critical choice to continue in sport or exercise or not.

This would seem to suggest that exercise and sport and the maximum use of the body is not part of our nature, and that students have not been given (a) adequate instruction in the totality of the body and the role of physical fitness in our mental and psychological development, or (b) sports and activities tailored to their person and personality.

It seems self-evident that the quality of one's life is determined by the state of one's health. From time's beginnings health has been considered the sine qua non of the good life. "When health is absent," wrote Herophilus, the physician to Alexander the Great, "wisdom cannot reveal itself, art cannot become manifest, strength cannot fight, wealth becomes useless, and intelligence cannot be applied."

Strong words, but this seems a poor argument in the current ineffectual campaigns against cigarettes and booze and drugs, lack of exercise.

Threats fail. Horror stories of future heart attacks, diabetes and strokes have predictably fallen on deaf ears. People are not inclined to do something just because it is good for them. Athletics in schools should be chosen on the basis of what the teachers would like to do themselves. This is the rule followed by James Herndon, author of *How to Survive in Your Native Land*. What you don't do, the students won't do, was what Herndon found out.

"Why should we assume that the kids would want to do a lot of stuff that we didn't want to do, and wouldn't ever do of our own free will?" he asks. "Does the math teacher go home at night and do a few magic squares? Does the English teacher go home at night and diagram sentences?"

What about the physical education teacher? What about the other teachers? Can't they bring to the student the vitality of the drama, the esthetics that they themselves get out of the sport? Can we find coaches who can make lifelong athletes out of their students?

We have forgotten that we are talking about play. We are dealing with one of the primary categories of life, one which resists all logical interpretation. Play has a deeper basis than utility. It exists of and for itself.

When we expose play to the function of promoting fitness and preventing heart attacks, we change its gold to dross. As countless fairy tales have told us, the choice of treasure over truth will always fail. What we need then is to conserve those mysterious and elusive elements of play which make it its own reward. We must remove anything that suggests practicality and usefulness. What we do must be fun and impractical and useless, or else we won't do it. If we become fit and impervious to heart attacks and all those other dread diseases, it will be because we don't care if we drop dead doing what we like to do.

We should be in sports not because they are practical but because they're not, not because we feel better but because we don't care how we feel, not because our fitness is increased but because we are so interested we don't even notice.

Play is the key. We all love to play. We like only the jobs that have a play element for us. Anything as practical as physical education or physical fitness is not going to get to first base with most of us.

★ *Touchstone:* "A Child's Christmas in Wales,"
Quite Early One Morning, Dylan Thomas

Dylan Thomas has combined in one list *examples* with *explanation* and *contrast* in his description of the Useful and the Useless presents he received at Christmas as a boy in Wales.

There were the Useful Presents: engulfing mufflers of the old coach days, and mittens made for giant sloths; zebra scarfs of a substance like silky gum that could be tug-o-warred down to the galoshes; blinding tam-o'-shanters like patchwork tea cozies and bunny-suited busbies and balaclavas for victims of head-shrinking tribes; from aunts who always wore wool next to the skin there were mustached and rasping vests that made you wonder why the aunts had any skin left at all; and once I had a little crocheted nose bag from an aunt now, alas, no longer whinnying with us. And pictureless books in which small boys, though warned with quotations not to, would skate on Farmer Giles' pond and did and drowned; and books that told me everything about the wasp, except why.

Go on to the Useless Presents.

Bags of moist and many-colored jelly babies and a folded flag and a false nose and a tram-conductor's cap and a machine that punched tickets and rang a bell; never a catapult; once, by mistake that no one could explain, a little hatchet; and a celluloid duck that made, when you pressed it, a most unducklike sound, a mewing moo that an ambitious cat might make who wished to be a cow; and a painting book in which I could make the grass, the trees, the sea and the animals any color I pleased, and still the dazzling sky-blue sheep are grazing in the red field under the rainbow-billed and pea-green birds. Hardboileds, toffee, fudge and allsorts, crunches, cracknels, humbugs, glaciers, marzipan, and butterwelsh for the Welsh. And troops of bright tin soldiers who, if they could not fight, could always run. And Snakes-and-Families and Happy Ladders. And Easy Hobbi-Games for Little Engineers, complete with instructions. Oh, easy for Leonardo! And a whistle to make the dogs bark to wake up the old man next door to make him beat on the wall with his stick to shake our picture off the wall. And a packet of cigarettes: you put one in your mouth and you stood at the corner of the street and you waited for hours, in vain, for an old lady to scold you for smoking a cigarette, and then with a smirk you ate it.

Don't tell. Show. Notice that none of these *Touchstones* contains unsupported generalities or abstractions. Abstract concepts—like creativity, sensibleness, usefulness, and uselessness—should not be unsupported assertions about a person or thing or idea. These assertions are valid only if they are conclusions drawn by the writer (and thus by the reader) after surveying the evidence: revealing, lively, specific, pictorial, concrete details developed in the body of the paper. It is not enough to say: "He was a coward." Give it flesh and bones:

> He pursued no moral cause with zeal, had no principles which he would risk having to defend. He had nothing to say on any subject, for fear of becoming the object of everyone's scorn. And, yet it was his very timidity for which everyone scorned him.

It is not enough to say simply, "He was a cold person;" make it real:

> He felt nothing but disdain for his daughter. Even now as she tried to share her grief with him at the prospect of losing the pony, he glanced at his watch, anxiously anticipating the afternoon's golf game.

Not only should you avoid unsupported abstractions and generalities, you should also steer clear of words like *excellent, magnificent,* and *outstanding;* these, too, are conclusions best left for the reader to draw based on the content of your paper. It is easy to use such "blanket words" as substitutes for the proof you need to provide. Never use vague terms like "several reasons," "a large amount," or "a significant increase" when you could, with some forethought or research, provide a specific number.

Keep in mind the questions you want to answer. As you can see, the body of your paper must not simply state your promise in several ways. Unless your message is so brief or so fascinating that it does not need to be substantiated, or unless the intended reader has some special reason for accepting confidently what you have written, then you must make your promise good. The major advantage to using the question-and-answer approach to focusing discussed in **Workshop I** is that it helps you avoid the pitfalls of unsupported assertions and repetitiveness. Using this method can enable you to see early in the writing process what the major divisions of your subject are. When you organize your paper as answers to basic questions, you may immediately notice that some answers are much longer than others. When this occurs, it usually means that some of your questions are actually sub-categories of other questions. If some of the information on your original list seems to answer no question in particular, first, check to see if it is general enough to be included in your opening or closing paragraph; if it does not fit in either of those places, you should consider it a digression, and omit it altogether.

Revision at this stage of the writing process is accomplished by deciding what to put in and what to leave out of the paper and by deciding when your divisions have been adequately developed. Once you have fully answered the basic questions, you can match them against the intentions you stated at the outset and determine if they are compatible.

Question + Answer = Paragraph. Many students have difficulty paragraphing the body of a paper; If you use the question-and-answer approach, you should not have this problem because each of the questions and their individual answers should become a logical point to divide the paragraphs in your paper. Certain details belong together because they answer a basic question about your topic. You have separated and developed these details apart from others by using whatever methods have seemed appropriate, until you felt that you had answered the question completely. Each paragraph, therefore, is a single step, complete in itself, toward fulfilling your promise to your reader. With this question-and-answer approach, you will not only have a clear understanding of paragraphing, but you will also be unlikely to wander off the subject or to under-develop the ideas you are addressing.

As a final word, the following analogy may be helpful in remembering the importance of the development stage of the writing process: the development process in writing is somewhat like the development process in photography. At first, only the most prominent details in the picture seem clear, but, if you have focused properly and have chosen an appropriate subject and the right development solution, soon a sharp, clear picture will come into view.

→*Honing In*←

Assignment 1:

By what method or methods would you develop the following topics?
- (a) stereotypical treatment of a specific group (women, persons engaged in a certain profession, teenagers) in television commercials
- (b) types of characters in soap operas, situation comedies, or police dramas
- (c) the meaning of justice, hope, responsibility, friendship
- (d) essential qualities of a quarterback
- (e) the harmful effect of some toys or of some television programs on small children
- (f) the noon scramble for the school cafeteria or for the nearest door at the final bell

Assignment 2:

Evaluate the following three student-written compositions for length and types of development used. Enclose in parentheses material you think needs further discussion and be prepared to explain why. Are there unsupported assertions? Paragraphs that answer no specific question?

Student Model A:

Soap Operas

Soap operas are the objects of more controversy than any other shows on television. In them we see various lifestyles portrayed, many of them immoral or amoral. They are probably the most important shows on television.

Soap operas show how purportedly typical families live day-to-day and night-to-night. This is where the problem lies. Many soap opera writers feel that using suggestive material is the easiest way to get viewers, and the more viewers the better. They present a distorted view of life—flagrant infidelity and widespread corruption.

Many people have tried to cancel such shows. But can you cancel one soap opera and not another? Do soap operas differ materially from situation-comedies and game shows? Can you ignore the popularity of such shows as evidenced in the ratings? Does the Second Amendment provide freedom of viewing and listening as well as freedom of speech?

Canceling even a single "soap" will have far-reaching repercussions.

Student Model B:

Student Government

Our student government is useless because the principal vetoes just about every proposal we make. For example, we suggested that we be allowed to play music in our student center, but we couldn't because it was considered "too disruptive."

Our school has a good reputation for its academic and athletic accomplishments and many students from other schools want to go here, but if they ever did, they would be shocked at some of our rules. For example, if any cans, food, or wrappers are left on the tables or on the floor of the student center, then the sale of foods in cans and paper will be stopped altogether. And the only time a student can get a parking permit is after the first term of the junior year. Some students live a long way from the school.

All schools need rules, of course, but only sensible ones. If our principal would be more reasonable and would allow our student government to do more decision-making, it could be an effective organization, but right now it isn't.

Student Model C:

The Essential Qualities of a Quarterback

The essential qualities a quarterback must possess are speed, agility, strength, and acumen. He needs strong hands because he handles the ball more frequently than any other player, and he must be able to throw a forward pass to completion when he is in the passing position. He must move with speed and grace when he carries the ball or looks for a pass receiver. In addition to calling plays, the quarterback must also block, for which he needs speed, strength, and courage. Overall, a quarterback must be able to respond immediately with accuracy and should be able to size-up in a split-second the opponent's defensive alignment, locate the weakness in it, and call a play which will penetrate the line.

Assignment 3:

> A. Examine the following two essays, especially noting the question that each paragraph seems to have been designed to answer. You should find clues to the nature of the question in the first couple of sentences of each paragraph where the topic is introduced. You will notice that these opening sentences are not generally stated as questions, although they sometimes are, just for variety.
> B. In "The Creative Heritage," why does Van Doren make a lengthier reference to Shakespeare than to other artists? What is the one essential quality of an artist, according to Van Doren? How does he use this quality to unify and develop the paper?
> C. In "The Sea and the Wind That Blows," is White's description of his first encounter with the sea a digression, or does it further develop the idea of the essay? Does the prolific use of sea and sailing terms detract or add to the development of the piece? Why did you answer as you did?

> *Essay 1:* "The Creative Heritage," by Mark Van Doren

>> Before the creative spirit can be communicated to the young, or to those of any age who do not have it yet, it must be defined with all possible care, lest it be misunderstood at the very outset. Misunderstanding in this case can be serious; indeed, it can be fatal to the spirit in question. And the commonest form of misunderstanding consists of supposing that man ever does create anything—that is to say, causes it to come into existence, brings it into being, or originates it. Man simply does not have that power, though sometimes he seems to think so. His genius and his glory lie in an altogether different direction: he is an imitator, not a creator.

To call him an imitator may seem to belittle him, but it might be well to consider whether any other creature can do even that. No other creature can. All creatures, including man, find themselves in a world they did not make and could not have made. And man alone is capable of comprehending what this means. He alone can see the world as something outside of himself which he can reflect in that unique mirror, his mind. It is a unique mirror in that it is more than quicksilver and glass. It studies, it penetrates, it sees parts of things in relation to one another; in the scientist it combines and recombines those parts so that something entirely new may seem to result. But it is not entirely new, any more than the so-called creations of the artist are entirely new—made up, so to speak, out of things that had no previous existence. The scientist and the artist are alike in that they begin with existence, and go on from there to imitations or reconstructions of it, which by their brilliance can blind us to the fact that nothing after all has been brought into being. All that has happened is that being itself has become clearer and more beautiful to us than it was before. This is a superb achievement, and it does not belittle man to claim that he is capable of it. Rather do we then perceive his ultimate, his incomparable distinction.

The greatest artists are the most lifelike: the best imitators of life. Their works, we say, are so much like life that they might be life themselves. But they are not life; they are like life, and it gives us happiness to realize that this is so. If Shakespeare is the best of poets, the reason surely is that he misses less than other poets do of the world he renders. We say he leaves nothing out; he sees everything in its full form and at its right value, and, finally, he causes what he sees, and what he makes us see, to glow with its own natural color. But he does not make us see what was never there. We had seen it too, over and over. The difference now is that we love it more, and behold it with a deeper intelligence. There is nothing new in Shakespeare except this beauty in everything, which he has helped us see more completely than we had considered possible. No man could have done more for other men.

Was Shakespeare, then, original? What would it mean to call him so? He has never in fact been paid the compliment, if compliment it is. Nor can he be imagined as ever desiring that it should be paid him. He would rather have been praised as true—true to the life he found himself living with others. He would rather have heard it said of him that he noticed his life in all of its particulars. He was the greatest of noticers. And the child or the youth who has ambitions to be an artist should be asked if *he* is a noticer. What we call creation is nothing but noticing—and then, of course, reflecting and rendering what has been noticed. But first of all, noticed. The artist has good eyes and ears and uses them as most of us do not. He uses them to observe and relish what is *there*, outside himself or in; for he notices too how his own mind works, and lets none of its operations elude him. Yet his own mind, being the human mind, is like all other minds, just as the world outside of it is the same world for us all. We did not make our minds any more than we made the world they have the gift to mirror. The most original artist knows this the most humbly, and is the most likely to wish that we would judge his works by their truth, comparing it to what we already know.

He is also the most willing that we should compare his account of life with the accounts of other artists. To the extent that he competes with them, he expects to be measured by a standard common to all artists, and this standard is the truth, the whole truth, and nothing but the truth. If originality means trying something that no one ever tried before and no one will ever try again, then comparison ceases to be possible. The good artist prefers to be measured for results that can be stated. He is not, of course, concerned in any of his works with the whole truth at once. Particular truth is his practical aim. And toward this end he has selected a form that he will make as perfect as he can. The best art comes out of many attempts by many artists to write the same poem, paint the same picture, compose the same symphony or song. As soon as this is done perfectly—by Shakespeare, by Congreve, by Mozart, by Rembrandt—the effort moves into another field. But it was a concerted effort on the part of many persons who accepted the same rules. The artist who triumphed was original only in the intensity and the fullness with which he realized the possibilities of the form. The form was before him, as his success will live after him.

A young person who wants to practice a given art should be convinced first that it is indeed an art. It is a way of imitating life, and there are demands which it makes upon anyone who woos it. The chief of these demands are knowledge and love, not only of life itself, but of the means men take to reflect it. The artist loves his art, too, and in his apprentice days learns to love the masters who preceded him in its practice. The artist imitates other artists, and surpasses them if he can. But he begins by trying what they tried, and the better the artists he imitates, the faster he will improve—as Keats did, once he discovered Shakespeare, Milton, and Spenser. Left to himself, Keats might never have been impressive. He might have gone on merely trying to express himself. The proper business of the artist is not to express himself; it is to express the world, and the dimensions of the world are most clearly seen in the works of great artists. We can make them clearer still, but that will be hard work. The good artist will not hesitate to undertake it. Nor will he feel that he loses anything by learning. He will understand that the more he knows about life, and about the art he is compelled to practice, the better he will be. Compelled is not too strong a word for the desire that moves him. The good artist is born as well as made: born with the desire to do what we find him doing. But he *must* be made. So he delights to learn. Granted that be might never have written a poem if he had never read one, or painted a picture if he had never seen one—granted this, he now proceeds as if he were free, as in fact he is, to be first in the field if he can. He will never be free to be first, however, unless he understands that he is also last—the last to try what has been tried by a long line of artists before him. He goes to school to his art, and likes it.

Imitation and learning. We learn about life, and we learn to imitate it. To communicate the importance of these essentials is the best way to inspire a beginning artist. For one thing, it may relieve him of certain terrors, lest creation be the mysterious, the magic process it is all too frequently represented to him as being. The only mysterious matter is that some of us have the desire to be artists and some do not. But given the desire, the next thing to understand is that knowledge plays an indispensable role in the formation of the poet, the painter, the sculptor, the musician. It has been said that the more a lawyer knows about everything, the better a lawyer he will be. And so of doctors, and divines, and statesmen. And precisely the same thing is true of artists. They do not start from scratch; they start by scratching—by peering, by digging, by diving and coming up again. Their art was there before them, just as life was, which they will now set out to render. Nor will they lose by being in a given case just one kind of artist instead of another. Nobody ever felt sorry for Shakespeare because he was nothing but a poet, for Rembrandt because he was nothing but a painter, for Bach because he was nothing but a musician. Each had his own way—but it was the way of others too—of learning all there was for him to learn. Or for him to make us learn. For it is well to remember how much we learn from the artists. What we learn is not absolutely new, but we learn it in the most delightful of senses. We recognize it. Which means that we know it again, and better; more deeply, more clearly, more humbly with respect to its power and beauty.

It was said a long time ago that there is nothing new under the sun. It could also have been said—and doubtless it was—that there is nothing newer than this morning's sunrise, or the infant born today. Life, which never changes, is always starting over. And so is any art. The newest poet may be the best. But we shall not say this of him if there is no basis for comparison with others. The basis is his knowledge of the thing he imitates and of the art by which that is to be done. Inspiration is largely emulation of the artists we adore. But first of all, there must be some artists we adore. We must know and love them before we can surpass them. And so with life. We must know and love it before we can imitate its grandeurs.

Essay 2: "The Sea and the Wind That Blows," by E. B. White

Waking or sleeping, I dream of boats—usually of rather small boats under a slight press of sail. When I think how great a part of my life has been spent dreaming the hours away and how much of this total dream life has concerned small craft, I wonder about the state of my health, for I am told that it is not a good sign to be always voyaging into unreality, driven by imaginary breezes.

I have noticed that most men, when they enter a barber shop and must wait their turn, drop into a chair and pick up a magazine. I simply sit down and pick up the thread of my sea wandering, which began more than fifty years ago and is not quite ended. There is hardly a waiting room in the East that has not served as my cockpit, whether I was waiting to board a train or to see a dentist. And I am usually still trimming sheets when the train starts or the drill begins to whine.

If a man must be obsessed by something, I suppose a boat is as good as anything, perhaps a bit better than most. A small sailing craft is not only beautiful, it is seductive and full of strange promise and the hint of trouble. If it happens to be an auxiliary cruising boat, it is without question the most compact and ingenious arrangement for living ever devised by the restless mind of man—a home that is stable without being stationary, shaped less like a box than like a fish or a bird or a girl, and in which the homeowner can remove his daily affairs as far from shore as he has the nerve to take them, close-hauled or running free—parlor, bedroom, and bath, suspended and alive.

Men who ache all over for tidiness and compactness in their lives often find relief for their pain in the cabin of a thirty-foot sailboat at anchor in a sheltered cove. Here the sprawling panoply of The Home is compressed in orderly miniature and liquid delirium, suspended between the bottom of the sea and the top of the sky, ready to move on in the morning by the miracle of canvas and the witchcraft of rope. It is small wonder that men hold boats in the secret place of their mind, almost from the cradle to the grave.

Along with my dream of boats has gone the ownership of boats, a long succession of them upon the surface of the sea, many of them makeshift and crank. Since childhood I have managed to have some sort of sailing craft and to raise a sail in fear. Now, in my seventies, I still own a boat, still raise my sail in fear in answer to the summons of the unforgiving sea. Why does the sea attract me in the way it does? Whence comes this compulsion to hoist a sail, actually or in dream? My first encounter with the sea was a case of hate at first sight. I was taken, at the age of four, to a bathing beach in New Rochelle. Everything about the experience frightened and repelled me: the taste of salt in my mouth, the foul chill of the wooden boathouse, the littered sand, the stench of the tide flats. I came away hating and fearing the sea. Later, I found that what I had feared and hated, I now feared and loved.

I returned to the sea of necessity, because it would support a boat; and although I knew little of boats, I could not get them out of my thoughts. I became a pelagic boy. The sea became my unspoken challenge: the wind, the tide, the fog, the ledge, the bell, the gull that cried help, the never-ending threat and bluff of weather. Once having permitted the wind to enter the belly of my sail, I was not able to quit the helm; it was as though I had seized hold of a high-tension wire and could not let go.

I liked to sail alone. The sea was the same as a girl to me—I did not want anyone else along. Lacking instruction, I invented ways of getting things done, and usually ended by doing them in a rather queer fashion, and so did not learn to sail properly, and still cannot sail well, although I have been at it all my life. I was twenty before I discovered that charts existed; all my navigating up to that time was done with the wariness and the ignorance of the early explorers. I was thirty before I learned to hang a coiled halyard on its cleat as it should be done. Until then I simply coiled it down on deck and dumped the coil. I was always in trouble and always returned, seeking more trouble.

Sailing became a compulsion: there lay the boat, swinging to her mooring, there blew the wind; I had no choice but to go. My earliest boats were so small that when the wind failed, or when I failed, I could switch to manual control—I could paddle or row home. But then I graduated to boats that only the wind was strong enough to move. When I first dropped off my mooring in such a boat, I was an hour getting up the nerve to cast off the pennant. Even now, with a thousand little voyages notched in my belt, I still feel a memorial chill on casting off, as the gulls jeer and the empty mainsail claps.

Of late years, I have noticed that my sailing has increasingly become a compulsive activity rather than a simple source of pleasure. There lies the boat, there blows the morning breeze—it is a point of honor, now, to go. I am like an alcoholic who cannot put his bottle out of his life. With me, I cannot not sail. Yet I know well enough that I have lost touch with the wind and, in fact, do not like the wind anymore. It jiggles me up, the wind does, and what I really love are windless days, when all is peace. There is a great question in my mind whether a man who is against wind should longer try to sail a boat. But this is an intellectual response—the old yearning is still in me, belonging to the past, to youth, and so I am torn between past and present, a common disease of later life.

When does a man quit the sea? How dizzy, how bumbling must he be? Does he quit while he's ahead, or wait till be makes some major mistake, like falling overboard or being flattened by an accidental jibe? This past winter I spent hours arguing the question with myself. Finally, deciding that I had come to the end of the road, I wrote a note to the boatyard, putting my boat up for sale. I said I was "coming off the water." But as I typed the sentence, I doubted that I meant a word of it.

If no buyer turns up, I know what will happen: I will instruct the yard to put her in again—"just till somebody comes along." And then there will be the old uneasiness, the old uncertainty, as the mild southeast breeze ruffles the cove, a gentle, steady, morning breeze, bringing the taint of the distant wet world, the smell that takes a man back to the very beginning of time, linking him to all that has gone before. There will lie the sloop, there will blow the wind, once more I will get under way. And as I reach across to the red nun off the Torry Islands, dodging the trap buoys and toggles, the shags gathered on the ledge will note my passage. "There goes the old boy again," they will say. "One more rounding of his little Horn, one more conquest of his Roaring Forties." And with the tiller in my hand,

I'll feel again the wind imparting life to a boat, will smell again the old menace, the one that imparts life to me: the cruel beauty of the salt world, the barnacle's tiny knives, the sharp spine of the urchin, the stinger of the sun jelly, the claw of the crab.

Assignment 4:

The following is an excerpt from an essay entitled "The Thrill and Magic of a Country Store" by John Parris. The excerpt is divided into paragraphs the way the article was printed in a narrow newspaper column in which the breaks were made *typographically* to aid the eye in reading and not *logically* at the end of thought groups. There are three major logical breaks in the article excerpt. Can you find them?

Uncle John never did have toys like they had in the stores at home.

But the things he stocked at Christmastime were better than the toys in the town stores.

Things that caught a boy's eye and set him to wishing.

Like Barlow knives with bone handles and two blades. Or the light No. 2 steel traps a boy needed to set up his own trap line for trapping muskrats and the like. Or jew's harps or harmonicas which were called French harps hereabouts.

But mostly, Uncle John's Christmas stock was made up of fruits and nuts, which he never carried except during the holiday season and which folks never bought or asked for except at Christmastime.

Oranges were still a rarity for most mountain folks even in the early years of my childhood.

As a matter of fact, when Mama was a young girl oranges were such a rarity that most folks believed they could only be bought at Christmastime.

This belief probably was fostered by the fact that merchants never displayed the golden fruit at any other season.

As a result, oranges were as symbolic of Christmas as popcorn ornamented Christmas trees or stockings hanging from the fireplace mantel.

And in Uncle John's store the oranges stood out like golden headlights. Folks who were short of hard cash brought in eggs and swapped them to him for oranges.

Somehow, my own memory of early childhood Christmases and the December days around Uncle John's store is associated with oranges.

And Uncle John saw to it that there was always an orange in my stocking when we spent Christmas with him at Uncle Jake's and Aunt Minnie's or at Grandma's and Grandpa's.

He never would let me have an orange before Christmas.

And being around the store with him and seeing the oranges, I just couldn't wait until Christmas morning.

But I did.

Assignment 5:

In your own writing, as you begin a new paragraph, turn the major question answered by that paragraph into a statement most of the time, just as writers Van Doren and White have done. The statement then becomes the topic sentence for that paragraph. Write topic sentences for paragraphs designed to answer the questions you prepared for Steps 1–5 for the Critical Angle exercise at the end of **Workshop I**. Save these sentences to use in Assignment 5 of the Critical Angle section below.

◤ *The Critical Angle* ◥

Assignment 1:

In **Workshop I** on page 6, Assignment 1, you read a first draft of the introductory paragraph for the following student-written essay using the question-and-answer approach to writing compositions. The following is the complete text of the composition. Which ideas mentioned in the opening paragraph were developed in the body of the paper? (The complete text of the other composition appears on page 47.)

My School

As I sit at my desk in this old building, Wilton High School, I am aware of its proud traditions and of my attachment to them. I have grown up at this school, so she is special to me. At graduation, I will be leaving behind here some people who have provided the bedrock of my life for a long time. There are friends here—adults and young people—who know me almost as well as my own family knows me.

Before long I will begin a new part of my life; I will enter another school. That fact both excites and depresses me. I will be glad to leave the routine of classes that has become monotonous and predictable and to make new friends and see new places. I will miss seeing my Wilton friends in the halls after class to discuss the weekend's activities. I will miss the feeling of "Wildcat spirit" and pride I felt when I walked down to the front of the auditorium to receive my varsity letters for swimming and for track, and when I marched with the band on the football field playing the school song.

As I think about going to a new school, being away from Wilton, sometimes I am frightened. Will things fall into place? Will I get used to snow and cold weather? Will I *really* make new friends? Right now I am not sure, and so I feel especially secure sitting here in this old familiar building.

I guess Wilton High will exist for me hereafter as memories in the yearbook and as visits I make to see old friends or to come to an occasional varsity game. It is hard for me to imagine how it will be. It is strange that, until now, I have never been truly conscious of what it means to be where and what I am. The anticipation of being away from Wilton High has caused me to be more aware of what it has meant to me.

Assignment 2:

Read the following draft of a composition entitled "Our Grandmother" and write a revised version following these directions:

   A. Increase the developmental details. For example, when *were* the good old days? Why did you not tire of hearing her tales about them? What *were* the hardships and funny experiences she told about? What more can you say about her appearance? About her photographs?
   B. Make clear a single, overall intended effect or focus.
   C. Choose a more appealing title.

Our Grandmother

My sister and I sat listening to our grandmother tell us about "the good old days." We have heard her stories many times, but we never really tire of them. She told us about hardships and funny experiences from the days when she was young.

We asked to see again the scrapbook of yellowed pictures of the house she lived in, her relatives, friends, and pets, and the school and church she attended. She told us of the pastimes and social activities of young people back then, such as playing practical jokes and making handcrafts. She even told us about telling ghost stories for fun and reminded us that back then people were very superstitious. She also told us about some folk medicine remedies they used. Grandmother has always liked to cook, so we asked her about the ways of preserving food and some of her favorite recipes.

As she talked I looked at her and wondered what she had been like as a young girl. Now she is very old and wrinkled. Soon her voice trailed off and after a while she stopped responding to our questions altogether and nodded off in a kind of private reverie. My sister and I tiptoed quietly away.

Assignment 3:

The necessity of development is not unique to theme-writing. It is essential in writing narration, too, and it is usually a gradual "thickening of the plot." A story is developed if conflict complicates a situation, thereby making it interesting reading, listening or viewing. Uneventful stories are undeveloped ones.

Narrative development may take the form of a victory finally won or of an encounter with violence or death. The daily news reports indicate that such complications make good news stories as well as good reading. Complications are also found in competitive sports and in most forms of entertainment, especially in movies and in serious television dramas.

Develop the plot of a story you have heard somewhere, perhaps from your parents or grandparents about their childhood or about your own. Use the following questions as your guide in developing the original story:

> What was the situation?
> How was the situation complicated?
> What was the climax or crucial point?
> How was the conflict or complication resolved?

Remember that the answer to each of the questions should require at least one paragraph in your story, because in each instance you are looking at a different aspect of the story. In this way, narrative development is similar to the development of the other forms of writing you have been doing.

Assignment 4:

This exercise will show how the effectiveness of a good, lively piece of writing can be killed by removing all developmental details. Rewrite a famous piece of literature, reducing it to platitudes and generalities. Get rid of all examples, analogies, statistics, reasons, descriptive words, analytical comments, definitions—supportive material of any kind. Have fun with this assignment: reduce a whole novel or an extensive document to a few lines, deliberately simplifying or misrepresenting complicated details. You might try using the sing-song nursery rhyme cadence or very short primer-style sentences. Here are two examples:

The Hobbit (I)
J. R. R. Tolkien

Bilbo leaves his country seat
("Bag End," Hobbit-hole) to meet
Thirteen wacky dwarves, named Oin,
Kili, Ori, Bofur, Gloin,
Balin, Dwalin, Thorin, Nori,
Fili, Bombur, Bifur, Dori.

Off they go on missions brave,
Goblins grab them in a cave,
Spiders, elves, a wicked troll
Bar the passage to their goal—
Misty Mountain and its riches
Guarded by a dragon (which is
Just another stereotype
In this kind of mythic hype).

There's a magic ring, of course,
And a final show of force
Where the baddies, overthrown,
Yield the fabled Arkenstone;
Bilbo scorns it, bless his soul,
He just craves his hobbit-hole.

So, despite its good intention
Here's a tale that lacks invention.
Hobbits speak a stilted jargon,
Humorless; and in the bargain
There's a most egregious slur—
Not one female character!
But unless you're just a snob, it
Might be hard to kick the hobbit.

The Raven
By Edgar Allen Poe

Raven lurches
In, perches
   Over door.
Poet's bleary
Query—
   "Where's Lenore?"
Creepy bird
Knows one word:
"Nevermore."

                from *ShrinkLits* by Maurice Sagoff

Assignment 5:

Look again at the introductory paragraph and the questions and answers you wrote for Steps 1–5 in the Critical Angle portion of **Workshop I**. Decide which of the answers should be developed further and which of the methods mentioned in this chapter—such as facts, examples, descriptions—would be the most appropriate. Can you use all of the ideas in your original list in answering the questions? Are any of them offtrack? Why?

Write out the answer to each question using whatever method of development seems best. You do not have to use the same method for each answer. You may also combine methods, just as some of the authors did in the *Touchstones*. Use the topic sentences you prepared for Honing In, Assignment 3 of this **Workshop**.

Writers at Work

A. From *Yesterday in the Hills* by Floyd C. Watkins and Charles Hubert Watkins, p. 163.

The first three sentences in this piece were omitted altogether because the idea in them, that local rivalries were a source of great interest, was implicit in the fourth sentence. Notice how much stronger the paragraph opens without the unnecessary and cumbersome explanation. From the revision, what other information did the authors consider including at first that they later deleted? Which constructions did they simplify or clarify by replacing with clearer, more economical ones?

~~The radio taught the hill settlements many things about the great world. Competitions in sports in the hills had always been intense local rivalries, person against person, school against school, settlement against settlement. The strong feelings were carried over into the interest in national sports.~~ The hill people were as much ~~involved~~ *interested* in the Dempsey-Tunney heavyweight title fights as they would have been if the two ~~great~~ fighters had ~~both~~ been local boys. Dempsey was the favorite of almost everyone. ~~in the community.~~ In his garage in Ball Ground Roy Cobb had a radio that did not require earphones. ~~Great numbers of~~ M/men and boys from the hills met at the garage to hear the fight. Sometimes the noise from the listeners was so great that they could hardly hear. ~~the~~

37

fight. They cheered, argued, and hollered, "I told you he'd do it," and "See, you was wrong." When Tunney won the fight ~~there was a moment of silence before the loud groan.~~ they left quiet and disappointed.

~~So many things had come to the country by the time of television that it was only an oddity. It did not create any sensational community reaction such as the phonograph and the radio had.~~

The Roosevelt administration, the bank holiday, the fireside chat, the NRA, the WPA, and changing times brought the world to the settlement. ~~Government began to be involved in the daily affairs of men. To some extent~~ All his life General Wheeler ~~lost his independence when he lost~~ had kept his gold ~~which he had kept~~ hidden and buried in tin buckets. ~~For the first time the government participated offensively in his daily life in some action other than drafting a man for war. General~~ He distrusted banks and paper ~~specie~~ money. When the gold was called in, ~~he~~ General was reluctant to give his up. It was his gold, he said, and the government did not have ~~the~~ a moral right to it.

♣ ♣ ♣

B. From *Yesterday in the Hills* by Floyd C. Watkins and Charles Hubert Watkins, pp. 49-50.

Notice how the description of Luraline Worsham and her bustle has been revised to reflect the flavor of the rural setting. The stuffing is described and people's actions and reactions are *recorded* rather than *reported*.

Some women wore a lot of petticoats with wide red bands sewed on the bottom. They spun thread and knitted stockings. A woman who had no sewing machine visited a neighbor to sew or did all her sewing with a needle and thread. Luraline Worsham made herself a bustle, and stuffed it with sawdust. Hubert Holbert hit her with the ball during a game of town ball and sawdust just flew all over the place. Hubert hollered, "Luraline, your bustle is a-leaking its stuffing!" And she throwed it in the bushes and said she'd just have to make out without it.

C. From *In Time and Place: Some Origins of American Fiction,* "Culture versus Anonymnity in *House Made of Dawn,*" by Floyd C. Watkins, pp. 146-47.

The idea in the deleted sentence has been incorporated into the sentence following it by using a key phrase, "the religious hunt for the eagle;" this eliminates an unnecessary reference to the hunt. Notice that specific ideas that did not contribute directly to the main point of the paragraph, that hunting is an intimate experience, are also deleted—references to "six pages," the "war in Korea," and "Al Momaday."

As much or more than racing, hunting brings man into the intimate contact with the various realms of the world—nature, the land, God. Man and God meet each other in the natural world. God grows things; man harvests. Pinones, edible nuts from a low-growing pine, and deer are "the gift of God." The Jemez in *House Made of Dawn* hunt eagles, rabbits, deer, bear; and often the hunt is communal, carried out in groups, as in Faulkner's "The Bear." During his confusion immediately after the war, Abel remembers the religious hunt for the eagle. But the heroic hunt belongs to Francisco: he remembers his solitary stalking of a bear "beyond the white cliffs and the plain, beyond the hills and the mesas, the canyons and the caves," (198). Momaday has derived his terrain from stories told him by his father, who once made an extended hunt to and behind the Blue Mountain, to territories he did not believe existed.

❖ ❖ ❖

Editor's Workshop III: The Big Picture

Have you ever tried to assemble something without a picture to guide you? Imagine trying to assemble a model car or a plane or to sew a dress or to put a jigsaw puzzle together without having an idea of how the finished product is supposed to look. In writing, your picture to guide the reader is just as important. Of course, you have made it clear in the opening paragraphs just where your paper is headed and you have made sure your information is appropriate and sufficiently developed, but if you do not assemble your composition parts into the whole picture you intended to show, your reader will be confused. The purpose of this chapter is to help you make patterns out of the thoughts you have developed so that your purpose will be clearly fulfilled.

Anthropologists and criminal laboratory technicians can draw or even reconstruct a whole person or animal, just as it probably existed, from only a few bones. This reconstruction is possible because these professionals have carefully studied their subjects and they know where all the pieces fit. They can envision the whole and the pieces in relation to it.

That is the way organization of a paper works, too. In other words, the well-organized paper can serve as a guide not only to the readers, but also to the writer. Once you have a plan of organization in mind, as you continue to think of or locate new information, you will know where the new thoughts fit in, or if instead, they represent a new category of ideas—new paragraphs. Your picture is assurance of what is usually referred to as *coherence,* and it is a quality essential to all good writing.

Three things you should avoid when you begin organizing. First, avoid dull, pointless beginnings. The longer the paper, the longer the introduction may need to be, but it should never be delayed very long. Nothing is quite so boring as having to plow through several pages before you know the point of a composition. Second, avoid surprise endings; only a few writers have been able to master those. Avoid writing yourself into a corner and coming finally to "and then I woke up." This kind of ending is often used by poor or unprepared writers to try to justify the illogical content of their papers and to avoid working out inconsistencies. In a well-written composition, there is absolutely nothing that has not been weighed and considered and finally deemed essential to the paper, and that includes the ending.

Third, avoid trying to organize your thoughts before you have enough of them and before you have a clear idea of where the paper is headed. The first two steps emphasized in this text, *focusing* and *developing,* are essential steps that must be completed before *organizing* can successfully be done. Writing a formal outline in order to write a paper is illogical. Outlining is an analytical process predicated on the assumption that you have some thoughts to organize. Most writers think as they write and they do both in a disjointed, often disconnected fashion. The "big picture" develops slowly.

You cannot know in what order you are going to write your thoughts ahead of time so that you can arrange them neatly as an outline. Instead, you think and write, rethink and rewrite, arrange and rearrange as you try to grasp the whole idea and as you try to fit your thesis and all of the information in support of it into a complete whole. The organization process should begin immediately after the focus and purpose have been developed. Sometimes, of course, the original focus simply does not survive the development stage because it was not defensible after all. When you find that you have finally settled on a purpose and have developed it as fully as you can, you will be faced ultimately with arranging your ideas in a logical fashion in order to communicate them to your readers and to fulfill or defend your purpose.

Find the right combination. There is an old argument that students sometimes use that goes like this: How can I look the word up in the dictionary if I do not know how to spell it? The common-sense answer is, of course, that you have *some idea* of how to spell it and you will just have to look around in that area of the dictionary until you hit upon the right combination of letters. Organizing a paper works in much the same way.

The first step in organization, like the first step in development, is to consider the nature of the topic itself. Does it naturally suggest any specific kind of organization? There are several "styles" or methods of organizing but perhaps the most popular classifications are the following: *chronological, spatial, logical,* and *associational.*

Most narratives and descriptions of processes, for example, require that you sustain a *chronological* order in the mind of the reader. This *does not* mean, of course, that you must always start from Day One or Step One and tell the events in exactly the order in which they occurred. It *does* mean that you must frequently remind your reader, through the use of key words or phrases, just when the events he or she is reading about did or should occur.

Descriptions of objects and places generally depend on *spatial* order—left to right, north to south, near to far. Explanations, especially of abstract ideas, may be developed in *logical* order, from the simplest, most obvious or familiar notions, to the less obvious or more complicated ideas. For example, a paper designed to persuade the reader on a controversial issue may begin with a safe, common ground of agreement and work up to the most volatile ideas by the end of the composition. Sometimes it is effective to pair related ideas or things in order to show their similarities and differences; public and private schools, intramurals and competitive sports, amateur and professional golf. Reports may also be subdivided into major categories. A report on golf, for instance, may be divided logically into a discussion of the rules, a description of the equipment, the kinds of courses one may encounter, and the major strokes involved in the game.

An order which is more difficult to follow and to master is *associational.* In this kind of composition, ideas and reverie are often stimulated by the recurrence of a familiar smell, sight, or other sensory trigger. For example, an old newspaper in the drawer of an antique dresser may inspire one to wonder about the first persons to use that drawer and what they might have stored there. An arrowhead or a fossil may call to mind the first inhabitants of the region where it is found.

The organization process involves a kind of thinking that is primarily classification. Some persons are better at ordering and classifying than others. This part of the revision process requires a different kind of thinking from that which generates ideas and verbalizes them, but it is equally important. This thinking gives shape to your paper and without shape, your message is likely to be missed. Whole paragraphs may need to be moved around, or omitted; transition words may need to be inserted to tie ideas together so that they follow each other with a sense of purpose. Otherwise, your paper may be perceived as lacking *coherence;* that is, it will have a lot of interesting, but unrelated, details.

Keep the main parts and the details in proper perspective. Subordinate ideas within each paragraph and within the paper itself. For instance, in a discussion of how a stereo system works, you would not want to represent the speakers, the volume control, the channel selector, and the power source as equally important components or as part of the same circuit. Improper subordination can confuse and mislead the reader.

Remember the order in which you place the ideas you have developed is of great significance in insuring that the right picture develops in the mind of the reader. For example, the last idea seals the final effect. A different order would have a different effect. If you append a humorous conclusion onto an otherwise serious piece, you jeopardize the serious effect you intended for the piece to have.

Maintain order with transitions. Your reader needs to know the order in which you have chosen to present your developed ideas, so you need to give guide-words along the way. Remember, the object in writing is to communicate, and your message will not get through if the signals are garbled. The guide-words along the way are called *transition words* or simply *transitions*. They move your reader along smoothly from idea to idea, paragraph to paragraph, beginning to ending.

Some transitions are obvious. They are simply words or phrases like "another reason is" or "in addition to this disadvantage, there is another more serious one" or "the most reasonable solution to this problem is." Other transitions are less obvious. They are repeated ideas or words or phrases that keep reminding your reader what your focus is. An even more subtle method of transition is that which reminds your reader of the structure of your paper—"to the left of . . .," (spatial) or "after his basic training in Texas . . .," (chronological); or "private schools, on the other hand,. . . ." (logical).

If the momentum of the paper is interrupted for any reason, the transition will pick it up again and prepare the reader to resume the initial progress. Interruptions usually occur as lengthy, detailed examples, anecdotes, or descriptions. In longer papers, you may need a sentence or two to get the paper back on track. Books often have transitional paragraphs or even transitional chapters.

Pay special attention to the ending. Not only is it your final impression, but it is your final chance to persuade, convince, or impress your reader. It must, above all, not be inconclusive or appear to be missing altogether. It must not sound as if you could think of nothing else to write so you repeated ideas from elsewhere in the paper. Your reader must gain from the conclusion a sense of satisfaction that the subject has been covered, that his or her questions have been answered, that doubts are resolved, that you got where you set out to go in your introduction. The best conclusions may even prompt the reader to read further on the subject. They should never include new information that should have been introduced in the body of the paper.

Hook your reader at the outset by making the direction of the paper clear. Then follow through logically in a clear, organized fashion and your reader will stay with you. Not only do you need organization to guide your reader, you need it to guide yourself as well. You must see the relationship of the information you have accumulated and developed before you can expect your reader to "get the picture."

Each of the following excerpts illustrates one or more of the major organizational patterns mentioned in **Workshop III**. Point out words, phrases, clauses, and sentences that signal the particular pattern or combination of patterns indicated.

★ *Touchstone:* "Foreword," *Step by Step Macramé,* by Milton Sonday

The Chronological Pattern

Interest in knots has ranged from the intricacies of Leonardo da Vinci's interlacings, outlining complex Renaissance theories, to the fanciful fringes and embellishments of the Victorian era. Many cultures, ancient and contemporary, have used knotting as a means of fabric construction or decoration. This includes ritual masks of tribal Africa and fringes on Mexican shawls. Perhaps the most vital heritage, however, has been that of the sailor. Sailors, who have spent their lives with rope, twine, and cord and their interlacings and fastenings, have named countless numbers of knots. They have spent endless hours tying knots as part of their livelihood and as a means of pleasure. Few are aware of the fanciful and creative forms knotted by sailors in their spare time.

⭐ Touchstone: "Ogeechee," Georgia Rivers (Articles from the Atlanta Journal and Constitution Magazine), by Andrew Sparks

The Spatial-Logical Pattern

If the Mississippi is Old Man River, Georgia's Ogeechee is a lady—mother, sweetheart, harlot, a beauty, and a plaything. The lady hardly earns a livelihood. Some Georgia streams work for their keep—generating electricity, carrying freight, backing up behind dams that fatten the rivers into great multi-purpose lakes. But the wild, unspoiled Ogeechee does almost nothing, like some pampered darling—which it is for fishermen.

The 250-mile-long river extends from Greene County southeastward to Ossabaw Sound, where it flows into the Atlantic Ocean between the islands Ossabaw and Wassaw. For much of its course the river is extravagantly beautiful. Touring the Ogeechee is an adventure in sight-seeing, and can be done two ways, by boat and by car.

By boat, paddling quiet as Indians or scooting along scaring terrapins with an outboard, you fathom the river's soul, meet its family of snakes, alligators, high-jumping silver mullet, and quick darting redbreasts. You glory in the beauty of its shining black water, and absorb the lady's perfumes—magnolias, bream beds, honey-suckle, and the rich smell of black muck drying in the sun. You glide through a moving, sun-splashed cathedral of arched oaks, gums, and bays. Willows hang green curtains at the windows and tall, fat-bellied cypresses edge out into the water. On the Ogeechee, riding the current, you flee from civilization into an almost uninhabited world, deserted except for an occasional fisherman.

By car, you see a very different river as you wind your way up from the coast to the old ferry sites, cross rattle-trap wooden bridges scarily labeled "Load Limit, 3,000 Pounds," and scoot over wide, smooth concrete spans of the big tourist arteries that cross the river—U. S. highways 17, 301, and 1. Along all the roads you find the people who inhabit the river lands. You meet the folks, past and present, who loved the Ogeechee best. . . .

As you go up the river, crisscrossing it on the highways, it seems that time piles up like driftwood about the old fords and landings. The Ogeechee, like any other river, is an attic, a catch-all of history, an anthology of fishermen's tales, a Boccaccio collection of characters who have lived upon it, fought and fished it, died, and risked their lives in its coffee-colored waters.

★ *Touchstone:* "My Room," Student Composition

The Spatial-Associational Pattern

When I am in my room, I am surrounded by symbols of myself. They remind me daily who and what I am. I can see that it is clearly my room because it is an extension of my separate selves. It symbolizes not only my private self, but also my public, and even my imagined self, as well.

My desk, my bookshelf, and the clock beside my bed indicate that I am a student, a hard worker and a thinker. My bulletin board says that I am a doer. Thumb-tacked to it are finite reminders of my activities, mental and physical: my hobbies, my vacations, and my school trips, my awards, my girlfriends. My dresser says I am decidedly a *human* being; clean clothes, warm blankets, and sheets are folded neatly in the drawers; my comb, my brush, and my cologne sit on the top, beside the mirror in which I can see myself.

But the room reminds me further that I am not just me—I am part of a family, too. There are symbols of me as a son: the bed all neatly made by my mother's gentle realigning hand and the article and books on business and economics I was inspired by my dad to read. The birthday cards lying on my desk are symbols of me, the brother. The dog hairs on the little rug by my bed left by my golden retriever who often greets me there, say I am a friend and a master. These symbols all together say to me, "I am loved."

My closet door stands ajar and in it I see a symbol of my mind, cluttered with unpursued ideas and projects left unfinished, incomplete schemes and dreams of the future. The dream of becoming an architect is there, among the drawings and crumpled cardboard creations. My dream of becoming a sculptor is hidden there in the heart of a deformed mass that never quite became a Santa Claus.

My radio and my bed are the items in my room that symbolize the way in which I nourish these and other dreams, for they represent my fantasies. I lie on the bed and listen and dream and all my dreams come true. I am handsome and talented. I am re-enacting all the exciting scenes in the theatre of my world and I am the star. And yet, with only one knock on the door, I can be jarred out of this fantasy and come back to the pressures of life.

My room is clearly mine because it is here that all of the parts of me are clearly defined; it is the one place that all of my selves co-exist in harmony.

★ *Touchstone:* from "A Child's Christmas in Wales," by Dylan Thomas

The Chronological-Associational Pattern

One Christmas was so much like another, in those years around the sea-town corner now and out of all sound except the distant speaking of the voices I sometimes hear a moment before sleep, that I can never remember whether it snowed for six days and six nights when I was twelve or whether it snowed for twelve days and twelve nights when I was six. All the Christmases roll down toward the two-tongued sea, like a cold and headlong moon bundling down the sky that was our street; and they stop at the rim of the ice-edged, fish-freezing waves, and I plunge my hands in the snow and bring out whatever I find. In goes my hand into that wool-white bell-tongued ball of holidays resting at the rim of the carol-singing sea, and out come Mrs. Prothero and the firemen.

It was on the afternoon of the day of Christmas Eve, and I was in Mrs. Prothero's garden, waiting for cats, with her son Jim. It was snowing. It was always snowing at Christmas. December, in my memory, is white as Lapland, though there were no reindeers. But there were cats. Patient, cold and callous, our hands wrapped in socks, we waited to snowball the cats. Sleek and long as jaguars and horrible-whiskered, spitting and snarling, they would slink and sidle over the white back-garden walls, and the lynx-eyed hunters, Jim and I, fur-capped and moccasined trappers from Hudson Bay, off Mumbles Road, would hurl our deadly snowballs at the green of their eyes. The wise cats never appeared. We were so still, Eskimo-footed arctic marksmen in the muffling silence of eternal snows—eternal, ever since Wednesday—that we never heard Mrs. Prothero's first cry from her igloo at the bottom of the garden. Or, if we heard it at all, it was, to us, like the far-off challenge of our enemy and prey, the neighbor's polar cat.

★ *Touchstone:* from "The Prologue," *The Family of Man* by Carl Sandburg

The Associational Pattern

If the human face is "the masterpiece of God" it is here then in a thousand fateful registrations. Often the faces speak what words can never say. Some tell of eternity and others only the latest tattlings. Child faces of blossom smiles or mouths of hunger are followed by homely faces of majesty carved and worn by love, prayer and hope, along with others light and carefree as thistle-down in a late summer wind. Faces having land and sea on them, faces honest as the morning sun flooding a clean kitchen with light, faces crooked and lost and wondering where to go this afternoon or tomorrow morning. Faces in crowds, laughing and windblown leaf faces, profiles in an instant of agony, mouths in a dumbshow mockery lacking speech, faces of music in gay song or a twist of pain, a hate ready to kill, or calm and ready-for-death faces. Some of them are worth a long look now and deep contemplation later. Faces betokening a serene blue sky or faces dark with storm winds and lashing night rain. And faces beyond forgetting, written over with faiths in men and dreams of man surpassing himself. An alphabet here and a multiplication table of living breathing human faces.

In the times to come as in the past there will be generations taking hold as though loneliness and the genius of struggle has always dwelt in the hearts of the pioneers. To the question, "What will the story be of the Family of Man across the near or far future?" some would reply, "For the answers read if you can the strange and baffling eyes of youth."

> There is only one man in the world
> and his name is All Men.
> There is only one woman in the world
> and her name is All Women.
> There is only one child in the world
> and the child's name is All Children.

→ *Honing In* ←

Assignment 1:

    Assume you have been assigned to write a composition on one of the following topics. What four or five questions would you want to answer in the body of your paper? What method of organization seems to fit your subject best? In what order would you answer these questions and why? How does the method affect the order?

    Topics: How to Make a (specific kind of) Sandwich
               Why (a particular actor or actress) Is So Popular
               Improving Your (name of a sport) Game
               Impressions of a Typical Family Dinner at My House
               Billboard Advertising Should Be Prohibited
               How to Play (a board or card game)
               An Important Purchase I Made
               I Can't Do Without (your own idea of a necessity)
               What It Means to Grow Up
               Reflections on Having An Older (or Younger) Sibling
               When I Learned to Be a Good Loser

Assignment 2:

    The following are two questions and the answers given by high school students in response to them. Which answers in each set represent primary goals and which represent subtopics of those goals? For example, Question I, #5, "To invest in property and stocks," is really a subtopic because it represents what one could do if one is "financially secure" (#3). How many paragraphs should be contained in the body of a composition on each of these questions?

    Question I: What do you think are the primary ambitions and goals of persons your age?

    Answers: 1. To have a happy family life
                    2. To be well-educated

3. To be financially secure
4. To help others
5. To invest in stocks and real estate
6. To travel extensively
7. To be well-informed about current events
8. To have a house with a tennis court
9. To support the arts
10. To have a satisfying religious commitment

Question II: What do you think are the primary reasons why a person needs a high school education?

Answers:
1. To make important social contacts
2. To be better equipped academically for college, and ultimately, for a career
3. To broaden one's interests and cultivate one's natural talents
4. To become a better citizen in order to make informed choices in political matters
5. To learn social skills that will enable one to get along with others and be better able to communicate with them
6. To develop the physical skills needed for sports and recreation and for general health and well-being

Assignment 3:

As a class or in small groups, brainstorm ideas for a paper on a recent local controversy. Decide on either a pro or a con stand and then, together, list what you think should be covered in the body of the paper (basic questions or issues to be addressed). Then study the list of ideas or questions and, individually, add to it any ideas you feel are not clearly expressed, and eliminate any you find inappropriate or unnecessary. Arrange the ideas in the order in which you think they should be discussed in the paper and be prepared to explain why you would choose this particular order.

At the next class meeting, exchange papers with another student who worked on the same controversy. How is your list different from that of your classmate? How do you account for this difference?

Assignment 4:

Part of Dr. Sheehan's essay from **Workshop II**, "Going Beyond Fitness," is reprinted below with key transitional words, phrases, and ideas italicized. Turn back to the original text on page 16 and see if you can find the transitions in the remainder of the piece. Remember to look both within paragraphs and between them. Look for obvious transitions and subtle ones. List any words or ideas that are repeated or that signal the order of the essay. Do not list words that can link ideas unless they actually do.

Most recreational directors, physical education instructors, and promoters of exercise-for-your-health *programs* feel much the same as the fellow who finds it difficult to give away five-dollar bills down Main Street. *People just won't believe it's for real.*

The *programs* they prescribe seem so sensible and so in keeping with our nature it is incredible that *people don't accept them*. But facts are facts and there is no use railing against them. *If the plane won't fly, there's no use appealing that the blueprints said it would. A bridge that insists on collapsing in defiance to all engineering theory will not respond to oaths and imprecations. Nor will our neighbors bestir themselves to physical activity* unless we find the *proper approach to the problem.*

This approach will have to go back to basics. Where did we go wrong and how can we fight it? How can men be *motivated* to do what's good for them? *Motivation* is the main factor in the continuation of any activity, and especially in adult athletics where there is *no longer the need to continue in compulsory school exercise and sports activity*. Indeed it is just that *transition period from school to work and marriage* which carries with it the critical choice to continue in *sport and exercise* or not.

This would seem to suggest that *exercise and sport* . . .

◤ *The Critical Angle* ◢

Assignment 1:

The focus or thesis of the following paper is clear: competition in the classroom is just as important as it has always been. The ideas are well-developed, but they are not well-organized. The student mentions both pro's and con's of competition—a good idea for logical organization of the topic—but does not discuss them separately. Rewrite the composition, using the same thesis, but improving the organization and order of discussion.

Competition is Alive and Well

Many years ago, competition between students was stressed almost daily in activities such as spelling bees and debates. Today, we stress competition in elections for student clubs and for class officers, and in achieving academic recognition such as making Honor Roll. Although competitiveness in a particular subject or sport could cause one to study harder or concentrate one's energies on one area more than on the others, this generally is not the case. A competitive person is usually one who strives to be his or her best in many areas.

Sometimes competitiveness between students causes the weaker or less competitive student to feel discouraged and to lag behind the others. Actually this is a good opportunity for the student who needs to improve his or her skills to learn from peers who are good models. Competition can enable a person to learn or become more skilled in a particular area than he or she would otherwise be.

Competition in the classroom can prepare one for the kind of atmosphere and environment in which most businesses operate. In fact, it is impossible to avoid competition in any field or career one pursues.

Although the activities that foster it have certainly changed, competition is alive and well in today's classroom.

Assignment 2:

Write a "memory paper" based on a traditional family event such as Christmas, a family reunion, Thanksgiving, your birthday, or a trip to a special vacation place. Use the *Touchstone* selection from Dylan Thomas's "A Child's Christmas in Wales" as a model.

You might begin with "One Christmas (Thanksgiving, family reunion, birthday, etc.) is so much like the other, that I can never remember whether. . . ."

Include those occurrences that are repeated every year ritualistically and those unique events that make certain years especially memorable. Include both happy and sad memories. Do not make your paper a haphazard, disjointed list, but rather, group the memories in whatever way seems best. Thomas's groupings in the rest of the piece were under general headings such as Useful and Useless Presents (*Touchstone,* **Workshop II**), playing games in the snow, the Christmas meal, the uncles and aunts, and caroling.

End your paper with a statement about what you think has made this event a tradition in your family.

Writers at Work

A. From "Odysseus' Adventures, Then and Now" by Marc Lipsitch, student (1) and "Commitment in Odysseus, in Modern Heroes, and in Us" by Michael Rubenstein, student (2)

Get to the point quickly in your first paragraph. Use your strongest, most uncluttered language there because the opening is critical to the success of the entire composition. Its purpose is to interest the reader in the point you wish to make and to provide information about just how you will prove that point. If the opening doesn't create immediate interest, the rest of the paper isn't likely to have a chance to. Do you usually finish reading an article or a novel that has a dull opening? The dramatic improvement in the following compositions on *The Odyssey* was achieved by rearranging and expanding on ideas already in the original drafts. The numbers indicate the order of ideas in the first draft and the final order in which those same ideas appear.

First Draft Introduction (1)

1 Many of the people and dangers Odysseus meets in *The Odyssey* are similar to those people meet today. *2* Because human nature has not changed since ancient Greek times, and because even many divine being*s* have human characteristics and personalities, the *3* primary ~~basic~~ situations Odysseus ~~gets into~~ *faces* are similar to some of those faced by people now.

Final Draft Introduction (1)

2 Human nature has not changed *much* since ancient Greek times. *T*~~Odysseus and~~ *Odysseus'* the people of ~~his~~ era interacted in much the same way as we do now. There are Circes ~~and Alcinooses,~~ Nausicaas and ~~and~~ Calypsos, ~~and~~ Penelopes and Clytaimnestras now just ~~as much~~ as there were then. Because of this universal ~~our common~~ humanity, ~~many of Odysseus' adventures have similarities to those of modern people. The Greeks of Odysseus' time are similar to the Western Europeans and Americans of today, but~~ the adventures with the Cyclops, Aiolos, the Circonians, and Helios' ~~animals~~ particularly lend themselves to comparison with modern situations.

First Draft Introduction (2)

Throughout his adventures Odysseus proves to be committed not only to returning home, but also to regaining his honor and nobility. It is this commitment that allows him to overcome anything that threatens his goals. Similarly, the commitments of modern heroes drive them to achieve their goals. It is important that we have such mental attitudes when we try to accomplish something difficult. Like Odysseus, we must not quail when confronted with dangers or temptation. Instead, we should face our problems directly in order to overcome or endure them.

Final Draft Introduction (2)

Odysseus faced problems directly in order to overcome or

endure them.⁴ Like him, people who wish to succeed must not quail when confronted with dangers or temptations.¹ Odysseus' commitment to returning home and to regaining his honor and nobility allows him to overcome anything that threatens his goals. ² Similarly, the commitments of modern heroes drive them on to achieve their goals.³ Thus, it is important that we have such strong mental attitudes when we try to accomplish something difficult.

B. "Blythewood," By Harriet Daugherty, student

No matter how interesting the details, they cannot create an overall impression unless they are organized. The house described in this composition was an excellent subject, but the first draft was not clearly organized and the details were not consistently developed.

Blythewood

There is a house in Clarkesville, Georgia, that my family visits a few times a year. It is called Blythewood. Its floors creak with age and the paint peels from the ceilings and walls. The balcony sways if too many people are standing on it, and the beds creak as much as the floors. In the kitchen there is a dumbwaiter. It has not been used in years and is broken. When my sister and I were younger, we used to be scared of Blythewood. As we grew and became used to it, though, a warm feeling surrounded us and

Blythewood. We got used to the large, echoing rooms, and were able to sit and play games and feel comfortable doing so. We did not mind so much the cold and creaking room in which we slept. We liked to play in the yard and swing from the trees. The vastness of the house no longer bothers us and we greet a chance to go to Blythewood with happiness.

Its streams and woods are still fun to play in. They are not as much a screen as they once were, though. When we are walking in the woods, instead of cresting a hill and seeing more woods, a freeway is in plain view. More homes are being built in that area. It seems that more people have found that a house in the Georgia woods is a warm place to be.

Here is the final draft, organized *chronologically,* as if one were arriving for a visit there with the writer:

Blythewood

There is a house in Clarkesville, Georgia, that my family visits a few times a year. It is called Blythewood. <u>As we arrive through the front gate,</u> we see tall pines and hemlocks standing on either side, their limbs reaching out to one another forming an arch high above us. The dusty road winds on for a fourth of a mile before it meets the flagstone driveway which leads to the front of the house. When we are nearer, we can see the front steps and the semi-circular porch with white wicker furniture on it. Past the front steps, when we finally stop and get out, for the first time a long, hazy blue range of mountains comes into view. On a perfectly clear day, the sky is so blue that the mountains seem a part of it.

As we wait for Dad to open the door with the old-fashioned key, we see the familiar cracking white paint and green shutters. We feel glad we have made the long drive here. The door opens and the old house releases a musty smell. My sister Ann and I run through the cold hall and up the squeaking stairs to get first pick of the bedrooms. We always sleep in the same one. The walls are pink and the curtains, white; in its day it might have been a cheerful room, but now paint peels from the walls and the ceiling as well.

After settling in, we go out to the balcony above the front steps. We cannot run, for the balcony sways if too many people even stand on it. From there we see the mountains again and breathe the cool, crisp air. Next, we go to the upstairs hall to read the names of the people who have visited the house since we were last here. Names are written upon the wall beside a line marking the height of that person and the date he or she was last at

Blythewood. Quickly, we add our names to the list, hoping they will be higher on the wall than at our last visit. Doing so, we sign Blythewood's unique guest book.

<u>We run downstairs</u>, the bannister swaying as we lean on it, to find Mother already setting things up in the kitchen. We spot the dumbwaiter, which serves its original purpose no longer, but rather only to spark a child's imagination. Ann and I used to pretend, actually sitting on it, that we were landing a plane or guiding a submarine down into the depths of an imaginary sea.

<u>We go through the kitchen onto another porch at the back of the house in order to reach the yard</u>. The gravel on which we play is not kind to bare feet. It is layered first with soft moss, then with spiny grass blades which protrude through the surface of the red clay; finally little spurs, not unlike sand spurs, sit atop the grass, waiting to stab a misplaced toe.

<u>A trip to Blythewood was not always greeted with joy</u>. When Ann and I were much younger, we were afraid of its creaking floors and huge rooms. <u>As we grew, our love for Blythewood grew</u>, and we got used to the echoing rooms and were able to sit comfortably in them playing games. We did not even mind so much the cold, creaking rooms in which we slept.

Blythewood's woods and streams are still enjoyable to us now, yet the woods are not as dense as they once were. When we are walking in the woods, instead of cresting a hill and seeing more woods, a freeway is now in plain view. It seems that more people have found, as we have, that an old house in the Georgia mountains is a warm and relaxing place to be.

Editor's Workshop IV: Cultivating a Becoming Style

You've developed the focus of your paper and organized the material in a logical sequence. Isn't this sufficient to communicate your message to your reader? Probably not. You revise and rework for two audiences at once: yourself and your reader. At this point, you have probably pleased only yourself. Many writers are tempted to turn in their papers at this stage in the writing process because they feel that adequate content and organization in themselves will insure successful communication. Unfortunately, this is not the case.

You will always sacrifice some of your freedom of self-expression in order to clarify your message. There are several serious distractions that can keep your reader from getting your message. In order to prevent them, you must have access to a thesaurus, a dictionary, a style manual, and a grammar book—the essential tools of a writer's trade. Just as a repairman needs specific tools and manuals in order to repair a car or an appliance or any other piece of equipment, you need them too. **Workshops IV and V** will assist you in learning to use these tools.

Develop word-consciousness. The reason that papers so often fail at this stage is because of the distraction of poor diction. There are few messages so compelling that they cannot be weakened, disguised, or hidden by the use of the wrong word, or by the use of the right word in the wrong place. To combat this weakness, you must develop a sense of word-consciousness. This is another of the special kinds of thinking indigenous to good writers. Words are the smallest tools of our trade and yet our messages depend almost entirely on our sensitivity to their meanings and our ability to get them to work together for us.

Naturally, some of your attempts to find the right word or image will fail. That is always the risk involved in experimenting and using your imagination, but in taking such a risk, you will be following in the path of anyone who has ever succeeded—and failed many times beforehand—in producing any creation worthwhile, whether that person is a painter, a scientist, or a writer.

Saturday Review Editor Emeritus Norman Cousins regards words as so powerful that he compares them to the bloodstream of society. He writes:

> Language is not just an instrument but an environment. It is a vital part of the philosophical and political conditioning of a society. Attitudes are tied to the power of words to ennoble or condemn, augment or detract, glorify or demean. . . . Few joys of the mind can compare with the experience of lingering over a well-wrought image or hovering over an evocative passage. ("Thoughts on Literature," *Saturday Review,* July 1981)

The biggest culprits are probably "fad words." These include the current slang and other words that we use in our casual conversations. They creep into our writing where they appear as cute, all-purpose or "blanket" expressions that convey very little substantial information because they are intrinsically non-specific. A deliberate attempt to be cute usually falls flat; unless you have discovered that you have a natural talent for writing humor, avoid it. Even words like *creative, lifestyle, image,* and *ecology* have become almost trite because they have become faddish. A single informal or humorous word or phrase used out of place in a formal paper calls attention to itself in a negative way and may alienate the intended audience.

Learn to use the dictionary and a thesaurus. The mark of a good writer is that he or she reaches for the right word—and finds it. A good source for specific words is a thesaurus. Look up the general idea, or several related ones, and you will find many specific subcategories from which to choose the one you have in mind. It can be disastrous to try to use the thesaurus in reverse—to search for an idea, rather than to lead you to a more specific one. If you misuse the thesaurus, you will probably choose an imprecise word that calls attention to itself because it doesn't quite fit.

In order to avoid such misuse, after you have located some words or phrases that might work for you, look each of them up in a dictionary in order to make the fine-line distinctions between synonyms that will help you narrow your choices appropriately. There are very few words that are really synonymous. Each word or phrase has a shade of meaning all its own; one word will rarely do the work of another.

Obviously, looking for the right words to send a message takes time and work. It is much easier to use familiar or blanket words out of habit. But we pay a high price for our laziness: boring or anesthetizing our readers.

Avoid smokescreens. At the other extreme from undue informality is pompousness. This style is evident when the writer mismatches diction and reader, or uses euphemisms or confusing constructions that hide the true meaning. Consider the following words or expressions that might be used because the truth is considered offensive, plain, unappealing or painful:

"fixed" instead of spayed or neutered
"put to sleep" instead of killed
"previously owned" instead of used
"terminated" instead of murdered

Many pompous expressions are verbal clutter words that really do not add anything to the meaning; many of them can be reduced to a word or two: "Due to the fact that" can be reduced simply to *because*. Euphemisms, passive constructions, and clutter words actually throw up a smokescreen between you and your reader; they detract from your message.

The words in a good sentence are pared to an optimum number; good writers leave in the words they need and they take out those that obscure their ideas.

One national company has enlisted the help of a computer to improve the diction in the writing of its employees. The Bell Laboratories in New Jersey have developed a computerized editorial system called The Workbench; it is a set of programs that will display a breakdown of what is wrong with an author's text. It was intended to help scientists express themselves in the clearest possible manner by eliminating clichés, wordy phrases, long rambling sentences, and jargon.

This is how the computer responded to "The Gettysburg Address" and the opening paragraph of *A Tale of Two Cities*. What is gained by the Workbench's analyses of these two famous works? What has been lost?

ABRAHAM LINCOLN
The Gettysburg Address

Fourscore and seven years ago our fathers brought forth on this continent, a new nation, conceived in Liberty, and dedicated to the proposition that all men are created equal.

Now we are engaged in a great civil war, testing whether that nation or any nation so conceived and so dedicated can long endure. We are met on a great battlefield of that war. We have come to dedicate a portion of that field, as a final resting place for those who here gave their lives that that nation might live. It is altogether fitting and proper that we should do this.

But, in a larger sense, we cannot dedicate—we cannot consecrate—we cannot hallow—this ground. The brave men, living and dead, who struggled here, have consecrated it far above our poor power to add or detract. The world will little note nor long remember what we say here, but it can never forget what they did here. It is for us, the living, rather to be dedicated here to the unfinished work which they who fought here have thus far so nobly advanced. It is rather for us to be here dedicated to the great task remaining before us—that from these honored dead we take increased devotion to that cause for which they gave the last full measure of devotion; that we here highly resolve that these dead shall not have died in vain; that this nation, under God, shall have a new birth of freedom; and that government of the people, by the people, for the people, shall not perish from the earth.

Workbench Analysis

Readability (years of education required): 10.8
Average sentence length: 26.7 words
Your average is very high. A good average would be 15 to 20 words.
Sentence types: simple, 10 per cent; complex, 40 per cent. Your document contains many more complex sentences than is common for this type of text. One way to improve this text would be to rephrase the most important ideas in simple sentences.
Passive verb phrases: 13 per cent

Revised Version

Eighty-seven years ago, our grandfathers created a free nation here. They based it on the idea that everybody is created equal. We are now fighting a civil war to see if this or any similar nation can survive. On this battlefield we are dedicating a cemetery to those who died for their country. It is only right. But in another sense, the task is impossible, because brave men, living and dead, dedicated this place better than we can.

Hardly anyone will notice or remember what we say here, but nobody can forget what those men did. We should continue the work they began, and make sure they did not die in vain. With God's help, we will have freedom again, so that the people's government will endure.

CHARLES DICKENS
A Tale of Two Cities

It was the best of times, it was the worst of times, it was the age of foolishness, it was the epoch of belief, it was the epoch of incredulity, it was the season of Light, it was the season of Darkness, it was the spring of hope, it was the winter of despair, we had everything before us, we had nothing before us, we were all going direct to Heaven, we were all going direct the other way—in short, the period was so far like the present period, that some of its noisiest authorities insisted on its being received, for good or for evil, in the superlative degree of comparison only.

Workbench Analysis

Readability: 46.1. A very high score for this type of document. Good training materials average close to the tenth grade level, even though the audience has more education than that.
Average sentence length: 119. The longest sentence is 119 words long. Sentences this long are frequently lists, which will be easier to follow if you convert them into list format.
Sentence types: simple, 0 per cent; complex, 100 per cent.
Passive verb phrases: 6 per cent

Revised Version

The times were the best and worst, wise and foolish. The era was one of belief and disbelief, light and darkness, hope and despair. Before us lay everything and nothing. We were all going direct to heaven or straight to hell. The period was so much like today that its loudest critics could describe it only in superlatives.

"Bell's Lettres" by
Natalie Angier
Discover, July, 1981

A third diction problem which can detract from your message is the use of the wrong word. Many words are often confused, such as *affect* and *effect,* because they resemble each other. This is not a simple spelling error; it is an error based on a misunderstanding of the meanings of the two homonyms. This problem will be addressed more completely in **Workshop V.** When you use one homonym when you should have used the other, look both of them up in the dictionary and make a note of what you find there. The next time you need to know the difference, you won't have to duplicate your effort.

Read good writing. There is a fourth quality or "minus factor" in word choice that may prevent your development and organization from working effectively. This is lack of *imagination.* Imagination is the most inconspicuous element that separates an interesting paper from a merely acceptable one. A good writer needs both skill and imagination. The work of a skilled writer who has little imagination is dull, but correct. The work of an imaginative writer who has few skills is lively, but chaotic.

The easiest way to describe an imaginative writer is to say that he or she is aware of the possibilities of our language; we all have the same words to work with. It is how we choose and arrange them that really matters. An imaginative writer not only senses the need for precision in diction, but also has a feel for the rhythm and imagery inherent in our language.

How can one cultivate imagination? Not by simply doing exercises in a book like this. The real cultivation comes in reading more imaginative writing. Other authors certainly cannot give you talent or experience, but they can, through their own measures of these factors, expose you to the possibilities for imaginative writing that you can extrapolate and pattern in your own writing. Because you can never remove yourself from your writing, whether it is a term paper or an essay, you can never remove the possibilities for using your imagination. You absorb a lot as you read the works of authors whose styles you enjoy and admire. That is the purpose of most of the models included in this text. Many of the skills you have acquired you learned by observing people who do something well. You learn writing skills the same way.

Borrow from the poets. One of the most efficient means of absorbing stylistic skills is through reading poetry. Poetry is quite different from prose, not only in how it looks and sounds, but also in the way it conveys meaning. Poetry is intimate and intense. In a recent interview, Robert Penn Warren described poetry this way:

> "The novel is a documentary of a kind; a poem is not. The novel is an account of a long trailing. A poem is aiming for the one-shot kill." ("Creators on Creating: Robert Penn Warren" by Carll Tucker, *Saturday Review,* July 1981).

Because a poem is "a one-shot kill," it communicates a sudden, powerful insight or feeling. A good poem is, most of all, a study in precise diction, the very quality that must be cultivated by good writers of prose as well. Because a poem is compressed the diction is extremely important. One of the most powerful tools of the poet's imagination is in the very root of a word itself; the poet, and the good prose writer as well, must learn to draw on the image inherent in the thing or the idea which is the subject of the writing. A poet has the power to see the message in terms of a thing or a situation which it is like. The poet often presents an image—a picture—which he links to his idea in order to help the reader to see the idea more clearly.

★ *Touchstone:* "The Dreamer" by William Childress

What are the *images* in the following poem? How are they linked to the *idea* of the child seeking refuge in a hiding place?

> He spent his childhood hours in a den
> of rushes, watching the gray rain braille
> the surface of the river. Concealed
> from the outside world, nestled within,
> he was safe from parents, God, and eyes
> that looked upon him accusingly,
> as though to say: Even at your age,
> you could do better. His camouflage
> was scant, but it served, and at evening,
> when fireflies burned holes into heaven,
> he took the path homeward in the dark,
> a small Noah, leaving his safe ark.

As you write, open yourself to the possibilities of metaphorical expression. It is a way of seeing that is often thought to be limited to poetry but which can serve the prose writer as well. The test of a good metaphor is this: can you see the picture suggested by the metaphor? If the picture is clear and makes sense, then the metaphor is a logical one. If the picture is ridiculous, it may be because you have "mixed metaphors," as in the following example: The fog had covered the roadway before us with its gray mantle, and then had slithered silently away.

"Slithered" is a verb which suggests snakes, but the fog is spoken of as "covering the roadway . . . with a gray mantle," which would suggest that the fog is being characterized as human.

The following two excerpts contain ideas that have been developed metaphorically. In both cases, the comparisons are effective because of the striking similarities that Huxley and Lincoln point out between the two subjects being compared. Notice, for example, how Huxley carries the analogy throughout the piece. His opening paragraph poses key questions based on the chess game analogy. Then, throughout the body of the essay, he continues the comparison by likening the world to a chessboard and man and woman to the players. The extended comparison leads finally to the analogy of education to "learning the rules of this mighty game" and showing it to be essential to "the life, the fortune, and the happiness of every one of us."

✶ *Touchstone:* from "A Liberal Education: and Where to Find It," by Thomas Henry Huxley, *MacMillan's Magazine*, XVII, March, 1868

Suppose it were perfectly certain that the life and fortune of every one of us would, one day or other, depend upon his winning or losing a game of chess. Don't you think that we should all consider it to be a primary duty to learn at least the names and moves of the pieces; to have a notion of a gambit, and a keen eye for all the means of giving and getting out of check? Do you not think that we should look with a disapprobation amounting to scorn, upon the father who allowed his son, or the state which allowed its members, to grow up without knowing a pawn from a knight?

Yet, it is a very plain and elementary truth that the life, the fortune, and the happiness of every one of us, and, more or less, of those who are connected with us, do depend upon our knowing something of the rules of a game infinitely more difficult and complicated than chess. It is a game which has been played for untold ages, every man and woman of us being one of the two players in a game of his or her own. The chess-board is the world, the pieces are the phenomena of the universe, the rules of the game are what we call the laws of nature. The player on the other side is hidden from us. We know that his play is always fair, just, and patient. But also we know, to our cost, that he never overlooks a mistake, or makes the smallest allowance for ignorance. To the man who plays well the highest stakes are paid with that sort of overflowing generosity with which the strong shows delight in strength. And one who plays ill is checkmated—without haste, but without remorse.

My metaphor will remind some of you of the famous picture in which Retzsch has depicted Satan playing at chess with man for his soul. Substitute for the mocking fiend in that picture a calm, strong angel who is playing for love, as we say, and would rather lose than win—and I should accept it as an image of human life.

Well, what I mean by Education is learning the rules of this mighty game. In other words, education is the instruction of the intellect in the laws of nature, under which name I include not merely things and their forces, but men and their ways; and the fashioning of the affections and of the will into an earnest and loving desire to move in harmony with those laws. For me, education means neither more nor less than this. Anything which professes to call itself education must be tried by this standard, and if it fails to stand the test, I will not call it education, whatever may be the force of authority or of numbers upon the other side.

★ *Touchstone:* "On Slavery" by Abraham Lincoln from a speech delivered at New Haven, Connecticut on March 6, 1860

If I saw a venomous snake crawling in the road, any man would say I might seize the nearest stick and kill it; but if I found that snake in bed with my children, that would be another question. I might hurt the children more than the snake, and it might bite them. Much more, if I found it in bed with my neighbor's children, and I had bound myself by a solemn compact not to meddle with his children under any circumstances, it would become me to let that particular mode of getting rid of the gentleman alone. But if there was a bed newly made up, to which the children were to be taken, and it was proposed to take a batch of young snakes and put them there with them, I take it that no man would say there was any question how I ought to decide. That is just the case. The new territories are the newly made bed to which our children are to go, and it lies with the nation to say whether they shall have snakes mixed up with them or not. It does not seem as if there could be much hesitation what our policy should be.

What are the impressions one gets from reading Lincoln's comparison of slavery to a snake? In what ways are we to interpret his statement, "That is just the case"?

Because poetry has its origins in song, much of it literally sings with rhythm. Rhythm, although not as obvious in prose, nevertheless, is an essential part of what makes writing easily readable. Rhythm in prose may be the result of the use of parallel constructions, which once begun, may become a very effective device, but which, if not continued, or if "mixed," may become as ludicrous as mismatched metaphors. The parallel elements may be single words, phrases, or clauses. They can be used to show how ideas are similar and to give a series of examples:

> We hold these truths to be self-evident, *that* all men are created equal, *that* they are endowed by their Creator with certain unalienable rights, *that* to secure these rights, Governments are instituted among men. . . .

Rhythm in prose may also be achieved simply as a result of sentence variety—a balance of long and short sentences, instead of a lot of choppy or artificially constructed ones. A series of short sentences may be used to suggest the workings of the mind of a fearful person. Long sentences may be used for description; uncluttered sentences may be reserved for reporting action. Often the best test of rhythm is how a paper sounds when it is read aloud.

Another simple tool of the poet, and one that prose writers might benefit from using, is the use of sharp visual or other sensory images. The more sensuous the language, the more it affects and moves us. The language itself may not even necessarily be altered; it may be only an occasional change in the usual word order that adds drama, audacity, or a surprise twist.

★ *Touchstone:* "Reminiscences of Childhood" by Dylan Thomas

In "Reminiscences of Childhood" Thomas describes the Welsh seatown where he grew up. Notice the poetic elements of his style. His vivid, precise diction is evident especially in his choice of verbs and adjectives, such as his description of the town as a "crawling" and "sprawling" one in which truant boys and old men "beachcombed, idled, and paddled." His imagery is sensual—especially visual—as he mentions the colors, sounds, feelings, and smells of his childhood memories.

The essay is remarkably readable—even the longer passages—because of the rhythm afforded by the balance of long and short sentences, the frequent parallel constructions, and the repetition of key words and ideas. Read aloud the passage that begins "Never was there such a town as ours" and hear the rhythm of his structure.

> . . . I like very much people telling me about their childhood, but they'll have to be quick or else I'll be telling them about mine.
>
> I was born in a large Welsh town at the beginning of the Great War—an ugly, lovely town (or so it was and is to me), crawling, sprawling by a long and splendid curving shore where truant boys and sandfield boys and old men from nowhere, beachcombed, idled and paddled, watched the dock-bound ships or the ships steaming away into wonder and India, magic and China, countries bright with oranges and loud with lions: threw stones into the sea for the barking outcast dogs; made castles and forts and harbours and race tracks in the sand; and on Saturday summer afternoons listened to the brass band, watched the Punch and Judy, or hung about on the fringes of the crowd to hear the fierce religious speakers who shouted at the sea, as though it were wicked and wrong to roll in and out like that, whitehorsed and full of fishes.
>
> One man, I remember, used to take off his hat and set fire to his hair every now and then, but I do not remember what it proved, if it proved anything at all, except that he was a very interesting man.
>
> This sea-town was my world, outside a strange Wales, coal-pitted, mountained, river-run, full, so far as I knew, of choirs and football teams and sheep and story-book tall hats and red flannel petticoats, moved about its business which was none of mine.
>
> Beyond that unknown Wales with its wild names like the peals of bells in the darkness, and its mountain men clothed in the skins of animals perhaps and always singing, lay England which was London and the country called the Front, from which many of our neighbors never came back. It was a country to which only young men travelled.
>
> At the beginning, the only "front" I knew was the little lobby before our front door. I could not understand how so many people never returned from there, but later I grew to know more,

though still without understanding, and carried a wooden rifle in the park and shot down the invisible unknown enemy like a flock of wild birds. And the park itself was a world of the seatown. Quite near where I lived, so near that on summer evenings I could listen in my bed to the voices of older children playing ball on the sloping paper-littered bank, the park was full of terrors and treasures. Though it was only a little park, it held within its borders of old tall trees etched with our names and shabby from our climbing, as many secret places, caverns and forests, prairies and deserts, as a country somewhere at the end of the sea.

And though we would explore it one day, armed and desperate, from end to end, from the robber's den to the pirate's cabin, the highwayman's inn to the cattle ranch, or the hidden room in the undergrowth, where we held beetle races, and lit the wood fires and roasted potatoes and talked about Africa, and the makes of motor cars, yet still the next day, it remained as unexplored as the Poles—a country just born and always changing.

There were many secret societies but you could belong only to one; and in blood or red ink, and rusty pocketknife, with, of course, an instrument to remove stones from horses' feet, you signed your name at the foot of a terrible document, swore death to all the other societies, crossed your heart that you would divulge no secret and that if you did, you would consent to torture by slow fire, and undertook to carry out by yourself a feat of either daring or endurance. You could take your choice: would you climb to the top of the tallest and most dangerous tree, and from there hurl stones and insults at grown-up passers-by, especially postmen, or any other men in uniform? Or would you ring every doorbell in the terrace, not forgetting the doorbell of the man with the red face who kept dogs and ran fast? Or would you swim in the reservoir, which was forbidden and had angry swans, or would you eat a whole jam jar full of mud?

There were many more alternatives. I chose one of endurance and for half an hour, it may have been longer or shorter, held up off the ground a very heavy broken pram we had found in a bush. I thought my back would break and the half hour felt like a day, but I preferred it to braving the red face and the dogs, or to swallowing tadpoles.

We knew every inhabitant of the park, every regular visitor, every nursemaid, every gardener, every old man. We knew the hour when the alarming retired policeman came in to look at the dahlias and the hour when the old lady arrived in the Bath chair with six Pekinese, and a pale girl to read aloud to her. I think she read the newspaper, but we always said she read the

Wizard. The face of the old man who sat summer and winter on the bench looking over the reservoir, I can see clearly now and I wrote a poem long long after I'd left the park and the seatown called:

The Hunchback in the Park

The hunchback in the park
A solitary mister
Propped between trees and water
From the opening of the garden lock
That lets the trees and water enter
Until the Sunday sombre ball at dark

Eating bread from a newspaper
Drinking water from the chained cup
That the children filled with gravel
In the fountain basin where I sailed my ship
Slept at night in a dog kennel
But nobody chained him up.

Like the park birds he came early
Like the water he sat down
And Mister they called Hey mister
The truant boys from the town
Running when he had heard them clearly
On out of sound

Past lake and rockery
Laughing when he shook his paper
Hunchbacked in mockery
Through the loud zoo of the willow groves
Dodging the park-keeper
With his stick that picked up leaves.

And the old dog sleeper
Alone between nurses and swans
While the boys among willows
Made the tigers jump out of their eyes
To roar on the rockery stones
And the groves were blue with sailors.

Made all day until bell-time
A woman figure without fault

> Straight as a young elm
> Straight and tall from his crooked bones
> That she might stand in the night
> After the locks and the chains
>
> All night in the unmade park
> After the railings and shrubberies
> The birds the grass the trees and the lake
> And the wild boys innocent as strawberries
> Had followed the hunchback
> To his kennel in the dark.

And that park grew up with me; that small world widened as I learned its secrets and boundaries, as I discovered new refuges and ambushes in its woods and jungles; hidden homes and lairs for the multitudes of imagination, for cowboys and Indians, and the tall terrible half-people who rode on nightmares through my bedroom. But it was not the only world—that world of rockery, gravel path, playbank, bowling green, bandstands, reservoir, dahlia garden, where an ancient keeper, known as Smokey, was the whiskered snake in the grass one must keep off. There was another world where my friends and I used to dawdle on half holidays along the bent and Devon-facing seashore, hoping for gold watches or the skull of a sheep or a message in a bottle to be washed up with the tide; and another where we used to wander whistling through the packed streets, stale as station sandwiches, round the impressive gasworks and the slaughter house, past by the blackened monuments and the museum that should have been in a museum. Or we scratched at a kind of cricket on the bald and cindery surface of the recreation ground, or we took a tram that shook like an iron jelly down to the gaunt pier, there to clamber under the pier, hanging perilously on to its skeleton legs or to run along to the end where patient men with the seaward eyes of the dockside unemployed capped and mufflered, dangling from their mouths pipes that had long gone out, angled over the edge for unpleasant tasting fish.

Never was there such a town as ours, I thought, as we fought on the sandhills with rough boys or dared each other to climb up the scaffolding of half-built houses soon to be called Laburnum Beaches. Never was there such a town, I thought, for the smell of fish and chips on Saturday evenings; for the Saturday afternoon cinema matinees where we shouted and hissed our threepences away; for the crowds in the streets with leeks in their hats on international nights; for the park, the inexhaustible and mysterious, bushy red-Indian hiding park where the hunchback sat alone and the groves were blue with sailors. The memories of childhood have no order, and so I remember that never was there such a dame school as ours, so firm and kind and smelling of galoshes, with the sweet and fumbled music of the piano lessons drifting down from upstairs to the lonely schoolroom, where only the sometimes tearful wicked sat over undone sums, or to repeat a little crime—the pulling of a girl's hair during geography, the sly shin kick under the table during English literature. Behind the school was a narrow lane where only the oldest and boldest threw pebbles at windows, scuffled and boasted, fibbed about their relations—

"My father's got a chauffeur."

"What's he want a chauffeur for? He hasn't got a car."

"My father's the richest man in the town."

"My father's the richest man in Wales."

"My father owns the world."

And swapped gob-stoppers for slings, old knives for marbles, kite strings for foreign stamps.

The lane was always the place to tell your secrets; if you did not have any, you invented them. Occasionally now I dream that I am turning out of school into the lane of confidences when I say to the boys of my class, "At last, I have a real secret."

"What is it—what is it?"

"I can fly."

And when they do not believe me, I flap my arms and slowly leave the ground only a few inches at first, then gaining air until I fly waving my cap level with the upper windows of the school, peering in until the mistress at the piano screams and the metronome falls to the ground and stops, and there is no more time.

And I fly over the trees and chimneys of my town, over the dockyards skimming the masts and funnels, over Inkerman Street, Sebastopol Street, and street where all the women wear men's caps, over the trees of the everlasting park, where a brass band shakes the leaves and sends them showering down on to the nurses and the children, the cripples and the idlers, and the gardeners, and the shouting boys: over the yellow seashore, and the stone-chasing dogs, and the old men, and the singing sea.

The memories of childhood have no order, and no end.

78   Thinking on Paper

★ *Touchstone:* from "A Christmas Memory" by Truman Capote

To which senses does Capote appeal in the following excerpt written in a vein similar to Dylan Thomas's reminiscence? How many examples of figurative language can you find?

It's always the same: a morning arrives in November, and my friend, as though officially inaugurating the Christmas time of the year that exhilarates her imagination and fuels the blaze of her heart, announces: "It's fruitcake weather! Fetch our buggy. Help me find my hat."

The hat is found, a straw cartwheel corsaged with velvet roses out-of-doors has faded: it once belonged to a more fashionable relative. Together, we guide our buggy, a dilapidated baby carriage, out to the garden and into a grove of pecan trees. The buggy is mine; that is, it was bought for me when I was born. It is made of wicker, rather unraveled, and the wheels wobble like a drunkard's legs. But it is a faithful object; springtimes, we take it to the woods and fill it with flowers, herbs, wild fern for our porch pots; in the summer, we pile it with picnic paraphernalia and sugar-cane fishing poles and roll it down to the edge of the creek; it has its winter uses, too: as a truck for hauling firewood from the yard to the kitchen, as a warm bed for Queenie, our tough little orange and white rat terrier who has survived distemper and two rattlesnake bites. Queenie is trotting beside it now.

Three hours later we are back in the kitchen hulling a heaping buggyload of windfall pecans. Our backs hurt from gathering them: how hard they were to find (the main crop having been shaken off the trees and sold by the orchard's owners, who are not us) among the concealing leaves, the frosted, deceiving grass. Caarackle! A cheery crunch, scraps of miniature thunder sound as the shells collapse and the golden mound of sweet oily ivory meat mounts in the milk-glass bowl. Queenie begs to taste, and now and again my friend sneaks her a mite, though insisting we deprive ourselves. "We mustn't, Buddy. If we start, we won't stop. And there's scarcely enough as there is. For thirty cakes."

The kitchen is growing dark. Dusk turns the window into a mirror: our reflections mingle with the rising moon as we work by the fireside in the firelight. At last, when the moon is quite high, we toss the final hull into the fire and, with joined sighs, watch it catch flame! The buggy is empty, the bowl is brimful.

→ *Honing In* ←

Assignment 1:

Write a one or two page paper in which you do the following:
(a) Identify a word most people over-use or misuse in speaking and in writing (see list below). Give several examples of how this word is abused; these examples may be exaggerated or humorous, if you wish.
(b) Give definitions of the abused word and illustrate its appropriate uses. Then suggest several synonyms that may be more precise than the abused word and show how they can be used.
(c) End your paper by using the abused word as many times in a *single* sentence as possible. This is intended to be a humorous or exaggerated concluding sentence.

ABUSED WORD LIST: awful, cute, crazy, fantastic, fine, funny, nice, sad, terrible, thing, wonderful

Assignment 2:

What is the overall impression of the diction in the following passage? What conclusion can you draw about the effectiveness of such writing? Rewrite the two paragraphs in a clear, objective style, avoiding all pompousness, slang, triteness, and clutter words:

They met for the first time last year on the set of one of the tube's longest-running, money-makingest sit-com's, introduced by movie mogul Vincent Aldrich. Overnite, they became the hottest twosome in Tinseltown. They bucked the theory that says you can't do business with friends and became best buddies offset as well as on. That really set tongues wagging.

All the lovey-dovey was thought to be history last week when the pair slugged each other on the set and then blew out of town to undisclosed separate locations to burn off the heat and nurse their respective wounds. This week, though gossip says the two are on the verge of splitting and the series is in danger of being dumped, fan mags are running pix of the reconsmiled pair.

Assignment 3:

Read the following excerpt from Chapter I of Charles Dickens's *Great Expectations* and answer the questions below.

> Ours was the marsh country, down by the river, within, as the river wound, twenty miles of the sea. My first most vivid and broad impression of the identity of things, seem to me to have been gained on a memorable raw afternoon towards evening. At such a time I found out for certain, that this bleak place overgrown with nettles was the churchyard; and that Philip Pirrip, late of this parish, and also Georgiana wife of the above, were dead and buried; and that Alexander, Bartholomew, Abraham, Tobias, and Roger, infant children of the aforesaid, were also dead and buried; and that the dry flat wilderness beyond the churchyard intersected with dykes and mounds and gates, with scattered cattle feeding on it, was the marshes; and that the low leaden line beyond was the river; and that the distant savage lair from which the wind was rushing was the sea; and that the small bundle of shivers growing afraid of it all and beginning to cry, was Pip.

A. 1. Give examples to show how the author has visually built up a sense of mystery, helplessness, and fear.
   2. What was the author's purpose in describing the area surrounding the churchyard?
   3. Describe what you would want an actor playing Pip to look like.
   4. What tone is established with the description of the weather?
   5. From whose point of view is this scene described? What effect does this have on the story? (Suppose the convict or an observer had told it.)
B. Write a one-page analysis of an excerpt of your own choosing in which the description is primarily visual. Point out both visual words and phrases and describe the probable effects the writer intended to produce in this excerpt by using these visual appeals.

Assignment 4:

To what extent does the effectiveness of the writing in E. B. White's "The Sea and the Wind That Blows" (**Workshop II**) depend on the diction? Point out especially effective word choices that make his ideas clear. To which senses does White appeal? What forms of imagery or metaphorical expression do you find?

◤ *The Critical Angle* ◥

Assignment 1:

Using either Dylan Thomas's "Reminiscences of Early Childhood" or Truman Capote's *A Christmas Memory* as a model, write an account of a memory from your younger days: a town, neighborhood, or house you used to live in, an older person who fascinated or puzzled you or whom you perhaps envied, a game or favorite fantasy in which you indulged, a vivid fear you had, acquiring or losing or playing with a pet or a friend (real or imaginary), a favorite hiding place.

You might begin with one of Thomas's statements, such as "Never was there such a town (neighborhood, house)." or with Capote's "It was always the same." Include specific sensory impressions and, if appropriate, some figurative language.

Assignment 2:

Write a two-or-three-page description of your room, emphasizing the qualities about it that make it uniquely yours. Use primarily visual description—colors, sizes, shapes, textures, appearances, movements. Make it clear what is in the room and how these things reflect your personality and preferences. If you wish, you may write about any room you have visited that has a special quality or feeling about it. It could be a hospital room or a waiting area (such as in an airport).

Assignment 3:

Choose one of the ideas below as the organizing principle of a descriptive paper in which you use an extended metaphor. Before you begin to write, make a list of all the words—nouns, adverbs, adjectives—that you associate with each of the two persons or things you are comparing. Include as many of these in your paper as are consistent with the metaphor.

Examine your completed draft to see if you have presented the two parts of your metaphor as having a number of features in common. Be sure the overall picture you want your reader to see—conceit, fear or frailty, for example—is clear.

Ideas:
1. A frail old person is like a turtle.
2. A two-year-old is like a monkey.
3. A deserted old house is like an abandoned castle.
4. An angry driver is like a bull.
5. A lost child is like a mouse.
6. A school is like a garden.
7. A conceited person is like a cat.

Writers at Work

A. Poetry, perhaps more so than prose, demands scrutiny for revision. Because the language of poetry is concentrated, it is usually shorter than prose and therefore appears deceptively easy to read and to write. If you have ever worked seriously on poetry, from either angle, you know this is not the case. Paring down the words so that only the strongest are left, trying different structures and line lengths take time and skill. The following questions were asked of three poets about a particular poem each had written:

    How did you get the idea for the poem?
    What changes did it go through?
    What techniques did you consciously use?
    Whom did you envision as readers?
    Would you say it has a paraphrasable meaning?
       If so, what is it?
    How do you think it compares with your other works?

Their responses will indicate how poets get ideas and how they polish them. The first two poets are students.

  I. Untitled

The girl bending at the waist
grasps the bar
with a tightened grip and
a white face, thin,
not painted yet,
hair pulled back and there's
nothing glamorous here,
but in her mind,
or in her someday,
or in her future mirror,
her bar is her rose,
and her costume is beautiful
and she cannot be seen
in the smudged window
frail
sweating
tired
surrounded by dirty bricks
above an empty street.

84   Thinking on Paper

The Poet's Response

I got the idea for my poem from a picture I saw of a young dancer in *National Geographic*. Sometimes pictures give me ideas to write on things I've never seen or experienced. The changes in the poem were mainly in the structure. For example, originally I wrote "in the smudged window
> frail, sweating, tired
>> surrounded by dirty bricks . . ."

Along with several such changes, I also added a line or two.

I tried to use vivid imagery in order to transfer the picture into the reader's mind as I saw it in the magazine. Also, the entire poem is purposely one sentence in order to keep the idea complete and continuous. I did not write with a particular kind of reader in mind.

The paraphrasable meaning that I see, although I did not write it with the intention of deep meaning, is the importance of goals and the motivation that they give. There is also an Ugly Duckling theme, in that there are implications that the girl will undergo a great metamorphosis.

Many people judge this poem to be my best, although it is by no means my favorite.

—Courtney Cook

II. A Catechism

Over the ages
i was born
Man has foolishly convinced himself
destined for success,
That realities can be created—
educated at the best schools
That the universe is structured and
in philosophy, psychology, theology.
Defined, somehow, through his Symbols.
i am a successful businessman,
Man seeks self-affirming through
am comfortably married,
Hollow rituals, never really seeing
have three children (chips off the old block),
Behind his ego-shield of self
pay my taxes,
Delusions. Perhaps this is what
and consider myself a devout Christian.
Separates him from God

The Poet's Response

I got the idea for this poem when I was reading in a book by Frank Herbert a passage about man's use of symbolism and ritual. I began to think about it and jotted down the lines of the poem which begin with capital letters on a piece of paper. After a few minor changes in word choice, I felt satisfied with the backbone of the poem, yet I realized it needed something to tie the abstract thought to reality. I then thought of the concrete examples—the even lines which do not begin with capital letters—and played around with organization for a while. The most important technique I used was the use of capitalization of lines to clearly differentiate between the two parts of the poem and to reflect, by capitalization, the more important part.

When I wrote this poem I envisioned no particular readers. I occasionally write poems for myself and then toss them in the bottom of my desk. Months after writing this one, I turned it in to Mr. DuPriest as a homework assignment.

This poem is unique in my writing, since all the other poems I have written tend to be more descriptive and less obviously philosophical. I like "Catechism," but sometimes I wish it were less choppy.

—Shannon Croft

III. The following response is from professional writer, William Childress, whose poem "The Dreamer" appears in **Workshop IV** on page 69.

The idea for the poem came, as almost all my poems, short stories, and articles do, from my own experience. As a child of eight I used to thread my way through seven-foot cat-tails fringing a millrace in the lovely Sierra mountain hamlet of Taylorsville to hide from my parents, and just to daydream in general. This was about 1940. In 1978 I revisited Taylorsville and found it astonishingly unchanged. Even the two-room shack my hand-milker father got free from the dairy still stood—but was now a storage shed. Cat-tails still abounded, and the slough itself was still intact.

The poem, as best I can recall, had no changes at all, and was one of those rare—rare to me anyway—birds that spring full-blown from the brow of inspiration. Obviously, the secret world I dwelt in at eight made a profound impression on me. I've since found that early experiences play a large part in shaping the adult person, especially in regard to the more imaginative professions. "Watching the grey rain braille the surface of the river" is a unique image and was sparked by watching a blind classmate in college touching the stippled dots in his books.

The conscious techniques I used were off-rhyme greatly and exact rhyme occasionally. Rhymes are off with BRAILLE CONCEALED, EYES/ACCUSINGLY, AGE/CAMOUFLAGE, EVENING/HEAVEN to avoid any singsong repetitiveness. I also consciously used syllabics, again to avoid a too-deadening rhythm. "Was scant but it served and at evening" is the sole 10-syllable line—the other 11 lines are all 9-syllable exactly, and I remember that deliberately setting the poem up syllabically helped me very much in choosing the words and images I wanted. So the changes were very slight, if any, other than correcting typo's or switching a word or two. Whereas, some of my poems take ages, this one took no more than an afternoon, with some final polishing later on. I'm getting a long poem ready for competition now called "The Ugly Baby," which had its beginning over two years ago.

Whom did I envision as readers? Me! Oh, that's silly—I wrote the poem for Philip Levine's poetry class at Fresno State College where I was then an undergraduate. It was very well received, and, of course, Levine was ecstatic when a very prestigious magazine, *Harper's*, accepted it. I'm reluctant to pontificate about poetry. To me, it's as much bane as blessing, since, alas, it has scant commercial or real value, and because it is a compulsive thing. Most poets are poets because they *have* to be. Even after I swear I'll never write another blankety-blank poem, I do. I think if a poem has any value it lies in its ability to touch some kind of identical chord in many different individuals, either through their own experiences which mirror it, or simply because in some way they "know where the poet is coming from." The fact that this poem is in 35 anthologies—college, high school, elementary—indicates something of that nature.

Paraphrasable meaning? Oh yes, I do think so. I see it as a retreat poem, in both the religious and the survival sense; retreating from the harsh reality of parents, demanding teachers or relatives, as well as a kind of monk's cell for meditation and dreaming and just trying to fathom the world at large. In the sense of complete isolation and shelter, there is probably a womb-like quality also. And although I've been an atheist since I first read the Bible at age 14, I am heavily steeped in religiousness, and use religious symbolism a great deal in all my literary writings. To me, it—King James only; I hate the dead flatness of the newer translations!—is a splendid repository of all that is fine and beautiful in English and I mine it very often. And have for 25 years of writing.

How does it compare with my other works? Ev Griffith, publisher of the important poetry newspaper *Poetry Now*, says I am probably the only poet to gain notice via just one poem! That's his way of poking fun at the fact that "The Dreamer" is in numerous anthologies while poems he considers superior, like "The Metamorphosis of Aunt Jemima" and "Lobo" are not. I think "The Dreamer" has some sort of innate appeal that makes kids identify with something about it. If a poem can do that, then it is worthwhile and comparable to works which might be thought "better" by some which do *not* have that quality. There are many Robert Frost poems of great excellence, but when he is quoted at all, it's usually from "Passing By Woods on a Snowy Evening." If a poem is *memorable*, if some part or all of it sticks in the mind—or in the craw—of the reader, then the poet has done well and ought to be pleased.

B. From "My Christmases" by Abbott Whitney, student

Because speech is spontaneous, it is repetitious and rambling. Since rough drafts are our efforts to write down our thoughts, they are quite likely to reflect the same problems as speech. One of the hardest stylistic tasks is to remove these undesirable traits from our writing, and yet retain the simplicity with which ideas are expressed. The following paper was revised almost entirely by omitting ineffective repetition that slowed the pace of the composition to a crawl. Read aloud both the original and the revised versions and you will hear the difference.

My Christmases

To me, no Christmas ~~of mine~~ is much different from the others, for it is a time when our family follows a ~~frequently used~~ traditional holiday routine. ~~during the Christmas holidays.~~ When I try to remember past Christmases ~~of mine~~, I am an investigator searching through my house for clues ~~or evidence of~~ to past Christmases ~~in order to get back memories.~~ When I do find ~~evidence of a past Christmas, usually~~ a toy or a stuffed animal, I almost drain the memories from it. ~~the object absorbing them into my mind.~~

Christmas in our family begins when my mother ~~takes out~~ hangs up our Advent calendar in which are various objects to be taken out one day at a time. My sisters will usually argue over who will get to take out the final item, a baby Jesus, on Christmas Day. Also, my sisters and I are always excited ~~the picking of a tree is a family event, for excitement is always~~

~~present~~ when we go to find what is to be the family Christmas tree. When we search for ~~our tree~~ *it*, we make sure not to crowd my father's head with too many possibilities, and we make sure that the trees we pick are at a reasonable price. Afterward, *though* we are always impatient ~~in leaving~~ *; we leave* the tree outside for a day or two before we ~~are able to~~ string lights on and decorate ~~the tree~~ *it*. When we are able to decorate the tree, my sisters will hurriedly place ornaments on the branches ~~of the tree~~, excited by what the tree ~~would~~ *will* look like after we finish~~ed~~ decorating it.

C. From "A Chat with Willa Cather," by Floyd C. Watkins and John T. Hiers, *Resources for American Literary Study,* Spring, 1979, p.35.

This piece became appreciably shorter when the revisions were made, starting with the title. Notice how the condensation has strengthened the ideas. "A Chat" is both shorter and more appealing than "A Recently Discovered Interview;" the editor is "pleased" instead of one who "must have been astounded:" an "atmosphere of uninhibited compatibility" becomes simply "congeniality." How many other revisions in the remainder of the piece resulted in stronger, shorter, or simpler statements? Other than condensation, what types of revision were made on this piece?

A Chat with Willa Cather

While visiting in her hometown of Red Cloud, Nebraska, in 1921, Willa Cather decided to drop into the office of the Webster County Argus for an informal chat. The editor, pleased by the impromptu visit, summarized the occasion in a remarkable article, a vignette of Willa Cather's close relationship to Red Cloud. This column, never reprinted, is neither a complete interview nor a haphazard recollection. Rather, it is an informal summary of their talks reported as indirect discourse. The human warmth and congeniality reveal something of Willa Cather the person. She remains, at heart, a citizen of Red Cloud and a lover of the prairie.

❖ ❖ ❖

D. From *In Time and Place: Some Origins of American Fiction,* "*As I Lay Dying:* The Dignity of the Earth," p. 186.

In this revision, sentences that made simple points were reconstructed simply, without repetition. Notice that this revision technique does not shorten the sentences, but it makes them considerably clearer.

In a mechanized world it is difficult to understand the complex relationship a farmer of the past had with his animals. How can a modern reader who does not know the difference between the commands *gee* and *haw* know what goes on between Jewel and his horse? Watching Secretariat on television provides no indication. Farm people know their animals. The Bundrens can tell who owns a pig by its breed. That spotted shoat floating down the river, they say, belongs to Lon Quick; he grows pigs like that.

The barn-burning in *As I Lay Dying* is not clear unless the reader knows, as Faulkner did, how farm animals act in a fire. When the fire is discovered, Jewel is the first to spring to action, and he wrestles a horse out of the barn. The contest is so furious that to Darl "They sound like an interminable train crossing an endless trestle." (209) A horse is so determined to remain in his stable during the excitement of a burning barn that no man can get him out without covering his head. That Faulkner has ~~Darl~~ [Jewel] to get the first horse out without a cover is ~~an incredible~~ [a high] tribute to ~~the~~ [his] strength and determination ~~of Jewel~~. Gillespie, knowing the nature of horses and mules ~~about~~ [in regard to] fire, uses his nightshirt and "stark-naked, his nightshirt wrapped about the mule's head, . . . beats the maddened horse on out of the door."(209) When Jewel and Darl knock a hole in the wall, the cow "rushes . . . through the gap . . ., her tail erect and rigid as a broom nailed upright to the end of her spine." (211) The comic simile accurately described a romping cow, and she rushes from the burning barn true to the nature of cows.

❖ ❖ ❖

E. From *In Time and Place: Some Origins of American Fiction,* "Culture versus Anonymnity in *House Made of Dawn,*" by Floyd C. Watkins, pp. 134–35.

This page represents revisions for clarity and style. For clarity, the author has added additional words or made the ones already there more specific. For a more readable style, he has combined sentences which are a continuation of the same idea by using compound subjects and a series of parallel constructions instead of a number of separate sentences with a lot of unnecessary detail to smokescreen the meaning.

The longhair Francisco journeys in his wagon toward the highway where he will meet his grandson returning from World War II. He [sets a snare to catch a beautiful bird for a prayer plume,] remembers how he raced over the road as a young man, sings and talks to himself about his later-arriving grandson,

Abel (using the diminutive, Abelito), and wears a new shirt for the welcome. Arriving at the place where the bus will stop, he hears the whine of tires, that "strange sound" of the other world; "it began at a high and descending pitch, passed, and rose again to become at last inaudible." Back comes Abel — — from the war and the other world, drunk. Francisco hides his tears, and laughs to create a facade of dignity, and loads the grandson into the bed of the wagon. Abel will leave again and attempt to come home again, and two other prominent Indian characters will try to resolve their own conflicts and Abel's over the differences between two utterly dissimilar cultures, between the old world of the Indian and the anonymity of the city.

From a narrow perspective *House Made of Dawn* is the story of a poor Indian who cannot find a place for himself. In broader terms, the novel is about man's loss of traditions, culture, past, community, fellow man, nature, religion, even meaning. The novel may satisfy vicariously the urbanite's longing for the vitality of the earth, for the old people living with each other in tribal and familial groups. A rootless world provides little place, or order, ceremony, for any man.

Customs, ~~and details and the furniture of life disappear. Even the~~ stories, and legends which gave a perspective on the communal life are forgotten. The twentieth century is a time of disappearances of cultures / without adequate substitutes. The wasteland of actuality stimulates the imagination to remember and preserve the richness of cultures not found in an anonymous world.

F. From "The Grandfather Clock" by Stephen Ahn, student

Descriptions of events can be made vivid by using words to indicate the one or two senses most dominant in a given situation. It is important to avoid writing too many sentences that begin "(the subject) *heard* or *saw* or *felt*" because such constructions are weak in comparison to those in which a verb, noun, or adjective tells what the subject has experienced. Verbs carry the most weight in the sentence and should be the primary carriers of the sense being emphasized. Never hide the action in a noun or an adjective when you can express it as a verb. Here is a first draft of a composition describing an event using auditory impressions.

The Grandfather Clock

~~The grandfather clock is about six years old. My mother bought it as a birthday present for my father. It towers at a height~~

Often, out of boredom from sleeping in our beds, my brother and I take sleeping bags into the family room and "camp-out" for the night. My brother, a very fast sleeper, usually leaves me in five minutes. I am a slow sleeper and sometimes may take up to an hour to just get drowsy. As I lie there after turning off the television set, I don't hear anything. Later, when my ears adjust to the silence, I hear everything. One of the most annoying sounds is the ticking of the grandfather clock my mother gave my father six years ago. Its large frame and heavy pendulum make its tick especially loud. Its monotonous thuds steadily drum and sometimes turn into bone-snapping clicks. Each click pierces my ears as I incorrectly anticipate the timing of the next one. Often it seems to tap at irregular intervals, a phenomenon which incites my imagination.

I imagine a ghost knocking on the window or blood dripping on the logholder in the chimney. Sometimes I cover my ears to keep from hearing the thundering shots from a cannon. Finally, at the gonging at the end of the hour, an atomic explosion tears my body in two as I cry out in terror. I can see nothing around me, but I sense a whirring mass and feel the vibrations of the explosion long after the last thunderous ~~round is detonated~~ detonation.

♣ ♣ ♣

G. From "Last Game" by Archie Roberts, student

The following composition about a crucial game in a hockey player's life is controlled by sound words that re-create the event.

Last Game

It started with a buzz. It grew louder and louder until it was deafening. He hit the clock and for a moment there was silence. It was the last time he would follow this daily routine. He took a cold shower and his limbs slowly woke up; the water booming on the walls and the floor around him kept him alert.

Only a few minutes later he would throw his uniform in the backseat and be ready to go. With a roar of the engine, he was on his way.

He got to the locker room right on time. Twenty minutes later he led the team out; the crowd was going wild. They knew it was the last time to see him in action. As he pulled the stick back, there was total silence. Then, with a loud crack, followed by a riot of cheers, he scored for two points in the first few minutes of play.

The second period allowed him to knock off only a quick pair, but he could not connect on anything else until early in the third period. The opponents, however, weren't doing much better, Soon it was tied at six; there was another period of total silence. Not even a breath could be heard in the arena. Three ticks were all that were left on the hands of hockey-fate. The puck was dropped with an incredible thud and with a swish of the stick, he scored, winning the game with an unbelievable pair of hat tricks.

Editor's Workshop V: Avoiding Mechanical Breakdowns

Clarity is a major goal in all writing. Striving for clarity begins with the first efforts to find a clear focus, and continues in later efforts to present fully developed and organized ideas using precise diction. All of these are means to the objective of communicating with other people. There is another kind of clarity that good writers pursue as well—*grammatical clarity*. Sentences must vary in length and structure so that they have a satisfying rhythm. They must be imaginative and free of verbal clutter, but they also must make sense.

Making sense of sentences involves a number of criteria which have already been discussed in the foregoing workshops. For example, each sentence must relate to the main topic and there must be no repetition that does not serve to contrast with or to emphasize what has gone before.

Grammatical clarity involves the mastery of standard grammar and usage. This means the elimination of run-on-sentences, errors in agreement, inconsistent tenses or viewpoints, incomplete sentences, rambling or incoherent sentences, inconsistent or inadequate or incorrect punctuation and capitalization, and misspellings. Errors of these kinds are not generally tolerated by readers because they are a reflection of the writer's lack of pride in his or her work. Writers who have not taken the time to read over and polish their work probably do not think the message is vital or worthwhile.

Drill exercises on these problems are readily available in any standard grammar book; if the explanations that follow need further clarification, or if you need practice exercises, consult one of them. While the problems listed are the ones that most often distract readers from the true purpose in a piece of writing, there may be others that are your particular problems. Remember, however, that the real test is not in your ability to do the exercises in a grammar text, but in your ability to transfer these operations to the process of rehoning your own sentences. Remember also that recognizing and eliminating these errors is simply proofreading, and proofreading is only one of the skills involved in the revision process; it cannot do the job alone.

1. INCOMPLETE SENTENCE (FRAGMENT)

A sentence is a complete thought; a fragment is only part of one, even if it begins with a capital letter and is followed by a period. Our conversation is full of fragments:

What do you think I should tell him?
Tell John I want to see him. Now.
Too late! The last mail pick-up for the day just left.

When we write narrative or descriptive passages that imitate thought or speech, we naturally use fragments; however, in expository themes, reports, and essays, we should avoid them. Make sure each sentence has a subject and a verb and is not dependent upon the preceding sentence or the following one to give it meaning:

EXAMPLES: (a) Sherlock Holmes noticed something else. *The tiny bruises on the lady's wrist that the cruel doctor had left there when he grabbed her.* (Appositive—fragment)

(b) We made our way back to class despite the cloudburst. *With dripping hair, sloshy shoes, and rain-drenched clothing.* (Prepositional phrase—fragment)

(c) A lot of unusual animals can be domesticated. *Pigs, for instance.* (Appositive—fragment)

(d) Our class was not required to take a mid-term test. *Because we voted to write a 1,000-word paper, instead.* (Dependent clause—fragment)

2. RUN-ON SENTENCE

Separate complete thoughts from each other with appropriate marks of punctuation or join them with connectives. *Do not use a comma to separate independent clauses, unless there are three or more containing parallel constructions:*

EXAMPLES: (a) I chose this car because it is inexpensive to buy, it is economical to operate, and it is fairly

comfortable to travel in. (Three independent clauses)
(b) Our team lost the first three games, at least two of these losses were attributed to penalty calls for clipping. (Run-on)
(c) Tryouts for the play are Monday and Tuesday, Wednesday night rehearsals begin. (Run-on)

It is generally preferable that you *do use a comma* when two independent clauses are joined by a coordinating conjunction (and, or, but, for, so, yet, nor).

EXAMPLES: (a) Our teacher is strict and business-like, *but* I do not think she is mean.
(b) We were too late to find a seat in assembly, *so* we sat quietly in the hallway.

When there is no conjunction or when there is an adverbial conjunction (consequently, furthermore, however, nevertheless, therefore), *use a semicolon.* Follow the conjunction with a comma. Further discussion of the semicolon is on page 107.

EXAMPLES: (a) Our first night at camp everyone went to bed early; we were exhausted. (No conjunction)
(b) The classroom was a mess; in fact, every desk had spattered paint on the writing surface and newspapers were scattered about on the floor. (Adverbial conjunction)

3. INCONSISTENCY IN THE USE OF PRONOUNS AND VERBS
Make sure each of your pronouns has a clear referent (antecedent).

EXAMPLES: (a) In Great Britain, it is traditional for *them* to have tea at 4 p.m. (For whom?)
(b) We are going to make up the rained-out match this Thursday afternoon, or forfeit it, *which* displeases some of the players. (What displeases the players?)
(c) The debaters nervously awaited a judgment as *they* tabulated each team's points. (Who tabulated the points?)

Make sure a pronoun agrees in number and person with its referent.

EXAMPLES: (a) When *you* finish a two-hour achievement test, a person is completely exhausted. (*You* are exhausted.)
(b) Our team lost every game *it* played away from home, but *they* won every game played at home. (A team works as *a unit,* not as a group of individuals.)
(c) *Every* cheerleader was doing *their* best to encourage the dispirited team. (A person can do only *his* or *her* best.)

Use the nominative case pronouns for the subject of a sentence or of a clause. Use the objective case pronouns as objects.

EXAMPLES: (a) The principal wanted to see Harold and *me* about making an announcement before assembly. (Objective case)
(b) Since Jennifer and *I* both had read *Huckleberry Finn* this summer, we decided to do our report on Mark Twain. (Nominative case)
(c) Shouldn't you or *I* attend the meeting? (Nominative case)

Do not switch verb tense or voice.

EXAMPLES: (a) Because we *spent* the entire morning looking for my car keys, no errands *were run.* (Shift from active to passive voice)
(b) So there I *was* in the middle of writing my lab report and he *wants me* to watch the dog's new trick. (Shift from past to present)

Make sure that the subject and the verb agree; this is especially important when the sentence is out of usual word order or when a number of words separate the subject from the verb.

EXAMPLES: (a) One of the stories has been omitted from the anthology. (*One* is the subject, not *stories*)
(b) There were not enough seats for all those who attended the meeting. (*Seats* is the subject.)
(c) How much does that sailboat cost? (*Sailboat* is the subject.)
(d) Every one of these cameras is expensive. (*One* is the subject.)

4. ERRORS IN CAPITALIZATION

Use capital letters with care. As a rule, do not capitalize the first letter of a word unless it is required by convention.

EXAMPLES: (a) Capitalize proper nouns and adjectives derived from them. *America, American; Allies, Allied forces*

(b) Capitalize the titles of offices and family relationships when they are used with names: Mayor Hobbs, Professor Johnson, Uncle Horace; *mayor* of *Greenfield,* our *professor,* their *uncle*

(c) Capitalize the names of geographical areas, but not the points of the compass: the *Midwest,* the *Orient, north* of a line from Knoxville to Asheville

(d) Capitalize the first and last words and all other significant words in a title. Use lower case for articles, prepositions, and coordinate conjunctions: *Tess of the D'Urbervilles*

(e) Capitalize the names of the days of the week, the months, and the holidays. *Do not capitalize the names of the seasons.*

5. MISSPELLED WORDS AND CONFUSED HOMONYMS

Many words are spelled the way they sound, but many more are not. In a handy place, such as on the inside cover of your notebook, keep a list of all the words you habitually misspell, so you won't have to look up the same word every time you need it. On your list, include the definitions of homonyms you may confuse such as the following: *whether* and *weather*; *loose* and *lose*; *their* and *there*; *accept* and *except*; *affect* and *effect*.

For the most frequently used words, try to devise a way to remember the troublesome part of the word. For example, if *friend* is a word that you usually misspell, perhaps you could remember that "a friEND is a friEND to the END." Or, if *believe* gives you trouble, try to remember one should "never beLIEve a LIE."

Finally, do not stop writing to look up a word. Instead, lightly circle the word or place a question mark or check in the margin at that line and later, when you have time, look up all the words about which you are unsure. This way, your spelling handicap can't interrupt your writing momentum.

6. PUNCTUATION ERRORS

Punctuation marks are like seasonings; while they do not alter the real substance of your composition, they enhance it and when they are applied too liberally, too sparsely, or incorrectly, they can make a crucial difference in the overall effect.

◼ *Touchstone:* from *Flowers for Algernon* by Daniel Keyes

The following excerpt is from Charley Gordon's diary; it recounts Charley's feelings on the day he learns that "Punctuation, is? fun!" Keyes uses Charley's profound misunderstanding of punctuation as an indication of his low intelligence level at the outset of the story. Flagrant violations of standard punctuation and grammar rules can seriously detract from the ideas being expressed. In this selection, Charley's violations control and override his ideas, and serve, instead, to characterize him as Keyes intended.

> April 6—Today, I learned, the comma, this is, a, comma (,) a period, with, a tail, Miss Kinnian, says its, important, because, it makes writing, better, she said, somebody, could lose, a lot, of money, if a comma, isn't in the right. place, I got, some money, that I, saved from, my job, and what, the foundation, pays me, but not, much and, I don't, see how, a comma, keeps, you from, losing it,
>
> But, she says, everybody, uses commas, so I'll, use them, too,,,,
>
> April—I used the comma wrong. Its punctuation. Miss Kinnian told me to look up long words in the dictionary to learn to spell them. I said whats the difference if you can read it anyway. She said its part of your education so from now on Ill look up all the words Im not sure how to spell. It takes a long time to write that way but I think Im remembering more and more.
>
> Anyway thats how come I got the word punctuation right. Its that way in the dictionary. Miss Kinnian says a period is punctuation too, and there are lots of other marks to learn. I told her I thought she meant all the periods had to have tails and be called commas. But she said no.
>
> She said: You, got. to-mix?them!up: She showd? me" how, to mix! them; up, and now! I can. mix (up all? kinds of punctuation—in, my. writing! There" are lots, of rules; to learn? but. Im' get'ting them in my head:
>
> One thing? I, like: about, Dear Miss Kinnian: (thats, the way? it goes; in a business, letter (if I ever go! into business?) is

that, she: always; gives me' a reason" when—I ask. She"'s a gen'ius! I wish? I cou'd be smart-like-her;
Punctuation,is? fun!

The Dash There are several marks of punctuation with which beginning writers may be unfamiliar. One way they try to cover up their inadequacies is to use a *dash* as a substitute for the marks they do not know how to use. The dash, however, like all the other marks, has a specific use. It represents a spontaneous interruption of one thought by another thought. It is an informal mark that must not be overused or used to do the job of another mark such as a colon or a pair of parentheses. It is typewritten as two hyphens, --. Examples of its correct usages are as follows:

1. The discussion of amendments to the dress code—a very controversial issue at our school—will probably not appear on the agenda at all.
2. The shuttle bus—if you should need to take it—runs every thirty minutes between the airport and our hotel.
3. At the play-off game, the referees were unable to stop the fans from—oh, you were at the game, too!

Underlining Another overworked mark is underlining for emphasis. When every paragraph has a few underlined words, the overall effect is weakened. No one word or idea stands out as more important than the others. Like the dash, underlining must be used sparingly. In print, italic type takes the place of underlining. Its proper use for emphasis is illustrated below:

1. I am never sure just how to spell the French word <u>liaison</u>; I frequently omit the second <u>i</u>. (Emphasis of a word or a letter)
2. "What do you mean, the vase I <u>used</u> to have on the piano?" Mother exclaimed. (Emphasis for voice inflection)
3. The drama class was in favor of presenting <u>The Boyfriend</u> at the spring play competition. (Indication of a title of a long work)

Quotation Marks Quotation marks are also often used without reason. If you are quoting someone or something exactly as it was spoken or written, use quotes. If you are in doubt, consult a good grammar book. Some correct uses are the following:

1. The subject of May Swenson's poem "The Centaur" is

a childhood memory of being a tomboy. (Indication of a title of a short work)
2. I know you said you wanted to "borrow" my pen, but that was last week and you still haven't returned it. (Indication of a quoted word being discussed)
3. My cousin's dog is very intelligent; he won't sit on command unless you say, "Sit, for a bone." (Indication of the actual words being quoted)

The Comma The comma is the most frequently used internal punctuation mark, but despite its rather simple uses, it is also the most abused. There are two very important rules that govern the use of the comma. First, use it to separate items in a series, but, if each adjective is equally stressed, do not use it to separate the adjective from the noun it modifies. For example:

American rock music is popular in many foreign countries as well as in the United States. (*American* and *rock* are equally stressed before *music*)

Second, if a pause is needed for clarity, use a comma; if two words or ideas belong together, omit it. For example,
1. Sports equipment, tools, umbrellas, boots, and old coats are all thrown haphazardly in our storage closet by the back door. (Pause between words in a series)
2. The man standing next to the librarian is the author who will read the essay. (No pause for a modifying phrase)
3. If you see the escaped ostrich, first, do not make him panic by running or making loud noises, and second, call the humane society or the police. (Pause for an interrupting transitional construction)

Parentheses Parenthetical information is usually set off with commas or with dashes, rather than with parentheses, because parentheses interrupt the momentum of the sentence and do not emphasize the words that are contained within them, as the other two marks do. Parentheses are used to add helpful but non-essential information to that contained in the rest of the sentence. Observe the different effects these marks have in the following examples:
1. Senator Sam Ervin (D., N. C.) chaired the Watergate investigation committee.
2. The merchandise in question (see enclosed letter) has already been paid for.

In a less formal context, commas or dashes might be used:

3. The merchandise in question, I am positive, has already been paid for.
4. The merchandise in question—a pair of slacks, a shirt, and a belt—was all paid for at the time of purchase.

The semicolon Halfway between the pause provided by the comma and the full stop for the period is the semicolon, which is composed of one of each of these marks. It means "stop briefly" and is used when a period could have been used but where two sentences should be joined because they are clearly related. For instance, the second sentence may contain a pronoun for which the antecedent is found in the first sentence, as in the following example:

All of the high school debate teams in the five-county area were invited to participate in the *tournament;* therefore, *it* was held in Columbus, a relatively central location.

It is also used to separate items in a list that contains commas, as in the following:

The franchise has its central office in San Francisco, California; its training center in Houston, Texas; and its shipping and receiving warehouses in Boston, Massachusetts.

The colon Another mark of punctuation that requires special use is the colon. Two of the main rules to remember about the use of this mark are that it precedes a list and it must be preceded by signal words that indicate that a list will follow, as in this sentence:

Among the essential items a camper needs are *the following:* a flashlight, a first aid kit, dry food, a change of warm, dry clothing, and a sleeping bag.

A less frequent but also important use of the colon is to signal that a specific bit of information or a thought will follow, as in this sentence:

Which famous story begins with this line: "Three dollars and eighty-seven cents"?

The Apostrophe The apostrophe is used in three ways. Its most common usage is to indicate the possessive of nouns and indefinite pronouns, as in the following examples:

1. The outcome of the investigation will be *anyone's* guess.
2. The coat on the chair is *Susan's.*
3. This is the *team's* second trophy this season.

NOTE: The apostrophe is *not* used to form the possessive of personal pronouns: *yours, its, ours, theirs, hers.* Also, if a plural

noun ends in *s,* an apostrophe follows it. A singular noun ending in *s* is usually followed by *'s*.
1. These are the *students'* papers.
2. A Christmas Carol is one of *Dickens's* most memorable works.
3. It was necessary to buy a two *months'* supply of groceries to stock the boat for our cruise.
4. It was difficult to get the *waitress's* attention in the crowded restaurant.
5. For the heroine in Sophocles' *Antigone*, preserving human dignity is worth defying the highest laws of the state. (*Sophocleses* might be considered difficult to pronounce.)

If the plural does not end in *s,* add *'s* to it, as with the singular:
1. Could you tell me if that store stocks *women's* shoes?
2. Were the white *mice's* reactions to the light related to the fact that they were albinos?

The second major use of the apostrophe is in contractions to indicate that letters or numbers have been omitted:
1. Because the trip is a long one, *they're* going to take an early flight. (they are)
2. *It's* still possible to buy tickets to tonight's performance of the play. (It is)
3. *Who's* going to tell Mom that we broke the candy dish? (Who is)
4. If *you're* not sure you can be there, perhaps I should ask someone else to fill in for me. (You are)

NOTE: Contractions are generally avoided in writing reports and compositions, except in accounts of informal speech.

The third major use of the apostrophe is to form the plural of letters, figures, signs, and words referred to as words.
1. It is difficult to read her handwriting because the *n's* look like *m's*.
2. Informal marks like *&'s* should be avoided in compositions and reports.
3. His phone number has four *3's* in it.

✪ *Touchstone:* "Shawn on Ross" from *Here at the New Yorker,* Brendan Gill

The following excerpt corroborates the ideas in this **Workshop** by showing the degree to which Harold Ross, founder and first editor of *The New Yorker,* revered grammar and mechanics as catalysts of clarity and sense:

> Ross was devoted to clarity and stood in awe of grammar. Poets, he recognized—with some displeasure—had to be ambiguous and obscure at times, but he saw no excuse for ambiguity or obscurity in prose. He wanted every sentence of prose in the magazine to be intelligible, and he struggled hard to achieve that aim. The words "fuzzy," "cloudy," and simply "unclear" turned up often in his queries. He also wanted impeccable grammar. This seeming fanaticism about clarity and grammar, I think, was a form of courtesy to the reader. He didn't want the reader to be stumbling around in the murk, or to have to take time to decipher what someone was trying to say, or to be distracted from what was being said by the faulty mechanics of how it was said. "We don't print riddles," he often remarked. And we don't. (Being a non-formulator, he would not have thought of it this way, but his high standards of accuracy were a token of his more important high standards of truthfulness. In the same way, his high standards of grammar were a token of his more important high standards of journalistic and literary content, and of style.) In a refinement of his effort to attain total clarity, Ross tried to do away with indirection in writing—particularly in factual writing. He did not want facts to come in one moment later than they should. He wanted the reader to know everything he should know at each step of the way, and not be taken unawares by information he should have had at an earlier point. He did not want a writer to say that a character took off his hat unless it had been established that the character was wearing a hat. I interpret this avoidance of indirection, too, as a form of courtesy. Moreover, he did not want a writer to raise questions of any sort in the reader's mind (synonymous with his own mind) without answering them—if possible, immediately: he did not want the reader to be, as he said, "tantalized." (He said, "A writer should never arouse curiosity without satisfying it"—and he was a man whose curiosity was easily aroused.) Finally, Ross asked for sense. He wanted everything in the magazine to make sense, to be rigorously logical. To assist him in his pursuit of clarity, grammar, and sense, he assembled a group of gifted editors who specialized in those matters.

→ Honing In ←

Assignment 1:

Gather as many of your old themes, reports, and test papers as you can find from any of your classes. Look them over to see if any of the following sentence structure errors were marked (or should have been marked). Write revisions of all weak sentences. Or, if you prefer, revise and improve the sentence structure of an entire theme, report, or essay-test answer.
   Sentence structure errors:
   (a) An incomplete sentence; may be marked *fragment, Frag* or SF
   (b) Two or more sentences run together; may be marked *run-on* or RO
   (c) An overly long, confusing sentence; may be marked *awkward,* AWK or K
   (d) Monotonous or choppy sentences; may be marked *repetitious, Rep,* or *choppy.*
See pages 117 and 118 for explanations of other marking symbols that may indicate sentence structure errors.

Assignment 2:

Randomly select any paragraph or two from a paper or report you have written and copy it, removing all punctuation and capitalization. Exchange papers with a classmate who has done the same assignment. What happens when you try to figure out the stream of unfamiliar words?

◢ *The Critical Angle* ◢

Assignment 1:

The following are two more excerpts from Daniel Keyes's *Flowers for Algernon* which were intended to show the difference between the retarded Charley Gordon who was to be experimented on and the brilliant—if only for a short while—Charles Gordon he developed into. What are the elements that Keyes used to mark Charley's "progris riport" as that of a retarded man? What are the elements in the letter that mark Charles Gordon as a genius?

Excerpt A:

progris riport 5 mar 6

They found my sister Norma who lives with my mother in Brooklin and she gave permission for the operashun. So their going to use me. Im so excited I can hardley rite it down. But then Prof Nemur and Dr Strauss had a argament about it frist. I was sitting in Prof Nemurs office when Dr Strauss and Burt Selden came in. Prof Nemur was worryed about using me but Dr Strauss tolld him I looked like the best one they testid so far. Burt tolld him Miss Kinnian rekemmended me the best from all the people who she was teaching at the center for retarted adults. Where I go.

Dr. Strauss said I had something that was very good. He said I had a good motor-vation. I never even knowed I had that. I felt good when he said not everybody with an eye-Q of 68 had that thing like I had it. I dont know what it is or where I got it but he said Algernon had it too. Algernons motor-vation is the chees they put in his box. But it cant be only that because I dint have no chees this week.

Prof Nemur was worryd about my eye-Q getting too high from mine that was too low and I woud get sick from it. And Dr Strauss tolld Prof Nemur somthing I dint understand so wile they was talking I rote down some of the words in my notebook for keeping my progris riports.

He said Harold thats Prof Nemurs frist name I know Charlie is not what you had in mind as the frist of your new breed of intelek** couldnt get the word***superman. But most people of his low ment**are host**and uncoop** they are usually dull and apathet**and hard to reach. Charlie has a good natcher and hes intristed and eeger to pleese.

Then prof Nemur said remembir he will be the first human beeing ever to have his intelijence increesd by sergery. Dr Strauss said thats exakly what I ment. Where will we find another retarted adult with this tremendous motor-vation to lern. Look how well he has lerned to reed and rite for his low mentel age. A tremen**achev**

I dint get all the werds and they were talking to fast but it sounded like Dr Strauss and Burt was on my side and Prof Nemur wasnt.

Burt kept saying Alice Kinnian feels he has an overwhelm**desir to learn. He aktually begged to be used. And thats true because I wantid to be smart. Dr Strauss got up and walkd around and said I say we use Charlie. And Burt noded. Prof

Nemur skratchd his head and rubbed his nose with his thum and said maybe your rite. We will use Charlie. But weve got to make him understand that a lot of things can go wrong with the experamint.

When he said that I got so happy and exited I jumpd up and shaked his hand for being so good to me. I think he got skared when I did that.

He said Charlie we werked on this for a long time but only on animals like Algernon. We are sure thers no fisical danger for you but there are other things we cant tell untill we try it. I want you to understand this mite fale and then nothing woud happen at all. Or it mite even sucseed temperary and leeve you werse off then you are now. Do you understand what that meens. If that happins we will have to send you bak to the Warren state home to live.

I said I dint care because I aint afraid of nothing. Im very strong and I always do good and beside I got my luky rabits foot and I never breakd a mirrir in my life. I dropped some dishis once but that dont count for bad luk.

Then Dr Strauss said Charlie even if this fales your making a grate contribyushun to science. This experimint has been successful on lots of animals but its never bin tride on a human beeing. You will be the first.

I told him thanks doc you wont be sorry for giving me my 2nd chanse like Miss Kinnian says. And I meen it like I tolld them. After the operashun Im gonna try to be smart. Im gonna try awful hard.

Excerpt B:

August 26—Letter to Professor Nemur (copy)
Dear Professor Nemur:

Under separate cover I am sending you a copy of my report entitled: "The Algernon-Gordon Effect: A Study of Structure and Function of Increased Intelligence," which may be published if you see fit.

As you know, my experiments are completed. I have included in my report all of my formulae, as well as mathematical analyses of the data in the appendix. Of course, these should be verified.

The results are clear. The more sensational aspects of my rapid climb cannot obscure the facts. The surgery-and-injection techniques developed by you and Dr. Strauss must be viewed as having little or no practical applicability, at the present time, to the increase of human intelligence.

Reviewing the data on Algernon: although he is still in his physical youth, he has regressed mentally. Motor activity impaired; general reduction of glandular functioning; accelerated loss of coordination; and strong indication of progressive amnesia.

As I show in my report, these and other physical and mental deterioration syndromes can be predicted with statistically significant results by the application of my new formula. Although the surgical stimulus to which we were both subjected resulted in an intensification and acceleration of all mental processes, the flaw, which I have taken the liberty of calling the "Algernon-Gordon Effect," is the logical extension of the entire intelligence speed-up. The hypothesis here proved may be described most simply in the following terms:

Artificially-induced intelligence deteriorates at a rate of time directly proportional to the quantity of the increase.

As long as I am able to write, I will continue to put down my thoughts and ideas in these progress reports. It is one of my few solitary pleasures and is certainly necessary to the completion of this research. However, by all indications, my own mental deterioration will be quite rapid.

I have checked and rechecked my data a dozen times in hope of finding an error, but I am sorry to say the results must stand. Yet, I am grateful for the little bit that I here add to the knowledge of the function of the human mind and of the laws governing the artificial increase of human intelligence.

The other night Dr. Strauss was saying that an experimental failure, the disproving of a theory, was as important to the advancement of learning as a success would be. I know now that this is true. I am sorry, however, that my own contribution to the field must rest upon the ashes of the work of this staff, and especially those who have done so much for me.

Yours truly,
Charles Gordon

encl: report
copy: Dr. Strauss
The Welberg Foundation

Assignment 2:

Try your hand at imitating the style, grammar and punctuation of someone else.
  (a) Write a recipe for chocolate cake as a five-year-old might write it and then as a gourmet cook might.
  (b) Pretend English is not your native language and write a

letter to your fictitious pen pal or pretend you are interpreting one he or she has sent to you.

Writer to Writer

1. Improving through Sharing

Good writing takes hard work and a lot of it must be done alone, but there is a kind of learning that comes through sharing with others. Look at the "Acknowledgments" section printed in the front of many books and you will find the names of numerous people who have shared in the preparation of the book: family members, students, colleagues, editors, friends, employers, and typists may all have shared significantly in bringing a book to completion. Professional writers care about their subjects, of course, but they also care what others think of their work. They seek honest appraisal in several areas along the way as they write. So should the rest of us.

For some of the assignments in this book you have been asked to share your work with another student in order to help you begin this kind of appraisal. Reading and critiquing each other's work is not the same as asking someone else to do your work, but rather it is asking someone to help you better understand how what you have written is perceived and how that perception may differ from your intent. If you consult with a classmate or a family member over your early drafts, you will be called upon to justify your word choices and the development and organization of your ideas. Sometimes you will not be able to justify them and you will find it necessary to express your ideas more clearly in another way.

You are quite likely to find yourself becoming more excited about your topic and to find it easier to generate new ideas as you continue to discuss your paper with an audience. The teacher is not the only one from whom you can seek advice. You may find a ready audience in a classmate, a relative, or a friend.

When you share those early drafts with someone else, do not worry so much about the quality of the writing as about the quality of the thinking. First drafts, remember, are hardly anyone's best efforts. Take turns reading each other's work aloud. Sometimes you can hear the mistakes better than you can see them.

As you rewrite further drafts of your paper, using what you have learned in these informal conferences, you will be conscious that your drafts are under scrutiny. We tend to want to look our best when we are under this kind of pressure—and this means not only improving the content, but also eliminating the ugliness of fingerprints, messy or incomplete erasures, and wrinkled pages. While these are not really internal revisions, they can certainly say something about the pride we take in our work and the seriousness with which we would like others to regard it. All of the sharing will pay off as you learn to short-circuit errors that are costly when they prevent the reader from getting your message.

The following questions are the kind you should try to answer as you evaluate another student's work, and of course, as you assess your own, although the latter is much more difficult to do than the former:

1. Can you state the *focus* of the paper in a single sentence? If you can't, then it probably doesn't have one.
2. Can you state the point of each paragraph or determine the *question* it was designed to answer?
3. Within each paragraph, which ideas are irrelevant? Where are necessary details omitted or insufficiently *developed*?
4. Can you tell where the paper is heading? Are there some passages that need to be switched around? If so, draw arrows or number the paragraphs in the correct order; or, if the paper is your own, cut the paragraphs apart and tape them together in the right *order*.
5. Does the composition read well? Is it rhythmical in sentence structure, precise and appropriate in *diction* and imagery, free of ineffective repetition or excess verbiage. Is the overall *tone* consistent with the ideas expressed and appropriate to the intended audience?
6. What *mechanical breakdowns* detract from the purpose of the paper? Mark them, referring if necessary to the chart that follows.

All of these questions are designed to assess what has gone well and what has gone wrong in a paper and to guide you in recognizing the remedy for the weaknesses. These questions pinpoint the major revising skills you have learned to use in this book.

II. *Putting Your Old Papers to Work*

Besides sharing as you write, there is a second way to improve: putting your old papers to work for you as you did on page 110 in one of the Honing In assignments. Do not throw them away, no matter how poor the evaluation.

REVISION GUIDE: INTERPRETATION OF MARKING SYMBOLS

The following chart is intended to help you make substantial revisions in your writing through the interpretation and remediation of the major composition problems indicated by the marking symbols most often used by teachers.

SYMBOL	MEANING	REMEDY
1. Arrow from one place to another	Word or idea out of place	Rethink the meaning of the word or sentence in question; check to see if the idea is out of place according to the order you have established in your paper
2. Awk/K	Awkward, unusual, confusing or artificial sentence structure	Restate the phrase or rewrite the entire sentence in *plain English*.
3. Fact?	Overstated, vague, or erroneous information	Check the text or primary source for exact reporting of material.
4. Fx (Further Explanation)	Development error or omission	Give more information; cite reasons, examples, details.

5. Logic/Clarity (CL)	Reasoning is unclear, unsound, or insufficiently stated	Supply *all* the necessary information to make your line of reasoning clear to the reader; make the necessary transitions.
6. Slang/Informal	Undue informality or use of a trite word or phrase	Avoid slang, ampersands (&), multiple punctuation (??? or !!!) and off-hand remarks to the reader. Do not use inappropriate abbreviations or excessive or multiple underlining.
7. Title of Paper	Title does not reflect contents of the paper or is improperly punctuated or missing altogether.	Choose an appropriate title; do not underline it or put quotation marks around it.
8. Rep/Wordy/Words crossed out	Ineffective repetition of the same word or idea	Economize for emphasis; eliminate weaker synonyms.
9. ¶ or no new ¶	Begin a new paragraph or do not begin a new paragraph	Remember the basic question each paragraph was designed to answer; begin a new paragraph for each new idea or major category of ideas.
10. Shift	Changing from one point of view or verb tense to another, or from singular to plural within the same composition	Finish your paper the way you begin it; keep the same point of view, tense and number throughout the paper.
11. Word Choice (WC) or Diction	Wrong word, ineffective choice of word, no such word	Check the dictionary to determine the authenticity of the word you have used.

Dig out old papers and keep a file of them. Keep a list of the symbols that appear most often and be sure you know what they mean and how to remedy the errors. Often a complete discussion of this information will be printed in your grammar or composition book; the Revision Chart is intended to serve as a guide in interpreting the symbols most often used to designate errors and in remedying the problems they indicate.

III. Understanding What the Grade Means

Each of the five **Editor's Workshops** has emphasized a specific quality that a good writer seeks to cultivate and some pitfalls to avoid. The lists below are designed to take the mystery out of how a teacher determines a composition grade. In fact, after having come this far, you should find that there is no mystery to the grading process at all: it is how well a writer cultivates these qualities and learns to spot these weaknesses in revision that directly determines the evaluation (grade) the paper merits. It is the writer—or rewriter—who determines the grade for himself or herself through the investment of time and energy that has already gone into the paper before it reaches the evaluation stage.

What is An "A" Paper?

1. It is focused on a significant thesis which is clearly and appropriately limited so that it can be covered in the length specified or suggested by the assignment.
2. The thesis is adequately developed and supported with significant, concrete, and relevant detail.
3. The paper is divided into logical paragraphs which are part of a clear orderly progression of ideas and in which ideas have been equally expanded on and developed with originality and consistency.
4. The paper has clear, natural, effective connections between paragraphs.
5. The style is appropriate for the subject; the sentences are rhythmic and effectively varied; the diction and the figurative language are fresh, economical, and precise.
6. The attitude or tone is consistent with the thoughts being expressed and appropriate to the intended audience.
7. The effectiveness of expression is not marred by the distraction of non-standard grammar or punctuation, or by misspellings,

What Is A "C" Paper?

1. The thesis is clearly expressed, but it is too general or uninteresting.
2. The thesis is supported with details, but they are occasionally repetitious, sparse, or irrelevant.
3. The organizing principle is apparent, but not adequately carried out; some paragraphs are developed more than others, some disproportionately to their importance.
4. The paragraphs are not unified by clear connectives, or, if present, the transitions are abrupt or monotonous.
5. The sentences are clearly constructed but lack variety and imagination; they are mechanically expressed.
6. The diction is clear, but uninspired. The paper may contain occasional lapses into slang or provincial language. The paper may be devoid of figurative language.
7. There will be occasional deviations from standard grammar and punctuation and some misspellings.

What Is An "F" Paper?

1. The central idea is unclear or unstated.
2. The supporting details are omitted, are not clearly relevant to the thesis, or are underdeveloped.
3. The organizational plan is not apparent, or is begun and not carried throughout the paper; ideas are repeated ineffectively.
4. The paragraphs are not unified; the transitions between them are unclear or ineffective.
5. The sentence structure and syntax are flawed. Fragments or run-ons appear frequently and ideas are awkwardly expressed.
6. Diction is wordy, vague, or non-standard.
7. Ideas are obscured by frequent spelling, grammar, and punctuation errors.